It Was a Miracle

A Memoir of Faith and Family on a Michigan Farm

Marvin "Bub" Nienhuis

Edited by Dean Kuipers

Photographs supplied by family, photographers unknown.

Cover design and book design by Chris Svensson

Published by Dean Kuipers, www.deankuipersonline.com

ISBN: (paperback) 978-1-7363886-0-0 (ebook) 978-1-7363886-1-7

FRONT COVER
Jack, Bob, Nancy and Roger's son Dave enjoy an O-So pop out in a freshly mowed hayfield. Notes on photo say, "1950 Oct 21, 2nd cut."

REAR COVER
Bub and Dot at a (probably Nienhuis) family reunion at Holland's Tunnel Park in 1938, the summer before they were married.

1928

Marvin "Bub" Nienhuis at eleven or twelve years old

6

PART I

Childhood

To one who always remained a comeback. It was said,
"and he certainly was a good fellow" – How could that be??

"And certainly he was a good fellow" – Chaucer
The quote accompanying Bub's photo in his high school yearbook

Without father and mother there could not be me and so this is how it all started.

My father Martin and I talked about a lot of things over the years but this first story impressed me the most, mainly because it had so much to do with me. He shared this experience with me for the first time when I was already in my twenties in order to console me when my dear wife and I lost our first child, which I will relate later. He was a wonderful father in this way, determined to give me hope and restore my faith that God's way was the best way.

The story went like this: shortly before my mother Nellie conceived me, she had become seriously ill with pleurisy. I was the sixth child to be born to my parents, and the doctor, Dr. Boone, was very concerned that she was so ill and then also with child. He told my dad he didn't think my mother was going to make it.

Dr. Boone had just come back from finishing his internship in World War I, not a religious man, but a very good doctor. My father, being a devout religious man, gathered my older brothers and sisters around the table at supper time and read Psalm 91 and prayed that all might go well for mother, being in the family way and being very ill at home. People didn't go to the hospital as they do now. He read:

He that dwelleth in the secret place of the most High shall abide under the shadow of the Almighty.

I will say of the Lord, He is my refuge and my fortress: my God; in him will I trust.

Surely he shall deliver thee from the snare of the fowler, and from the noisome pestilence.

He shall cover thee with his feathers, and under his wings shalt thou trust: his truth shall be thy shield and buckler.

Thou shalt not be afraid for the terror by night; nor for the arrow that flieth by day;

Nor for the pestilence that walketh in darkness; nor for the destruction that wasteth at noonday.

A thousand shall fall at thy side, and ten thousand at thy right hand; but it shall not come nigh thee.

Only with thine eyes shalt thou behold and see the reward of the wicked.

Because thou hast made the Lord, which is my refuge, even the most High, thy habitation;

There shall no evil befall thee, neither shall any plague come nigh thy dwelling.

For he shall give his angels charge over thee, to keep thee in all thy ways.

They shall bear thee up in their hands, lest thou dash thy foot against a stone.

Thou shalt tread upon the lion and adder: the young lion and the dragon shalt thou trample under feet.

Because he hath set his love upon me, therefore will I deliver him: I will set him on high, because he hath known my name.

He shall call upon me, and I will answer him: I will be with him in trouble; I will deliver him, and honour him.

With long life will I satisfy him, and shew him my salvation.

Die in de schuilplaats des Allerhoogsten is gezeten, die zal vernachten in de schaduw des Almachtigen.

Ik zal tot den HEERE zeggen: Mijn Toevlucht en mijn Burg! mijn God, op Welken ik vertrouw!

Want Hij zal u redden van den strik des vogelvangers, van de zeer verderfelijke pestilentie.

Hij zal u dekken met Zijn vlerken, en onder Zijn vleugelen zult gij betrouwen; Zijn waarheid is een rondas en beukelaar.

Gij zult niet vrezen voor den schrik des nachts, voor den pijl, die des daags vliegt;

Voor de pestilentie, die in de donkerheid wandelt; voor het verderf, dat op den middag verwoest.

Aan uw zijden zullen er duizend vallen, en tien duizend aan uw rechterhand; tot u zal het niet genaken.

Alleenlijk zult gij het met uw ogen aanschouwen; en gij zult de vergelding der goddelozen zien.

Want Gij, HEERE! zijt mijn Toevlucht! De Allerhoogste hebt gij gesteld tot uw Vertrek;

U zal geen kwaad wedervaren, en geen plage zal uw tent naderen.

Want Hij zal Zijn engelen van u bevelen, dat zij u bewaren in al uw wegen.

Zij zullen u op de handen dragen, opdat gij uw voet aan geen steen stoot.

Op den fellen leeuw en de adder zult gij treden, gij zult den jongen leeuw en den draak vertreden.

Dewijl hij Mij zeer bemint, spreekt God, zo zal Ik hem uithelpen; Ik zal hem op een hoogte stellen, want hij kent Mijn Naam.

Hij zal Mij aanroepen, en Ik zal hem verhoren; in de benauwdheid zal Ik bij hem zijn. Ik zal er hem uittrekken, en zal hem verheerlijken.

Ik zal hem met langheid der dagen verzadigen, en Ik zal hem Mijn heil doen zien.[1]

The family prayers were answered. Mother recovered, and soon after that it was time for me to be born. But apparently, things didn't go as well as they should have. Dad mentioned the procedure that was taken at that time: it may sound terrible, but the doctor advised bouncing mother on the floor, which was done between my dad and him. Whatever they did, it was near Christmas on December 22, 1916, that my mother gave birth to a son, Marvin Nelson. That was me. Marvin meaning "lofty" and Nelson meaning "son of Nell." Probably that is why it came to be Bub for short.

I suppose a lot of nice things were said about that little Christmas baby, but for some reason I don't remember.

I do remember some things that happened when I was quite young.[2] Of course, World War I ended in 1918 and I recall some of the songs that were sung, such as "When Johnny Comes Marching Home" and "Over There." I do remember going places with the horse and buggy, sometimes even traveling to Holland which was quite a ways to go, but everybody traveled that way. It took all day. My family had to deliver sugar beets we grew to the Holland St. Louis Sugar Company, which was a very successful business selling sugar during the war and after. I can still feel the vibration riding over the hard cement road while the horses were trotting at a good pace. We took our lunch along, as we couldn't afford to stop at restaurants those days. I even remember what we had: homemade bread with fat and brown sugar. During the winter, we did our traveling by sleigh. Everybody liked that, and when we took the sleigh to our regular church, South Olive Christian Reformed Church, it would be full of people by the time we arrived. Church was well attended and appreciated very much in those days, considering how we had to get there.

Dad bought our first car, a new, yellow, 1918 Nash Touring. I remember well sitting on the lap of the salesman, a man named Pete Lievense. I would have been two or three years old. I think him being nice to me might have influenced the sale. The Nash Touring was a beautiful car in those days. It was swell in the summer, but in the winter the radiator had to be drained and side curtains put on for the cold. Those snap-on curtains were canvas, with see-through plastic windows, and ice would form on them. I remember coming from Uncle Hank and Aunt Nettie's[3] on the Ninth of May, 1923, in such a heavy snowfall it took us hours to go home. No windshield wipers. I was six years old and I sat on the lap of Henry Timmer, my oldest brother's friend. I guess my oldest brother Eildert, who we called "El," was about seventeen years old at that time. We kept warm by wrapping ourselves in blankets, because there was no heater in the car. Very seldom would you go anywhere without tire repair: our Corduroy brand cord tires were good for about 5000 miles at the most. I remember that snow because it went on record as one of the latest spring storms ever experienced around here.

I recall another weather event, as well: a very bad storm on a Sunday afternoon while I was being cared for at home by my older sister Gladys and the rest of the family was in church. I was three years old, and a hail storm came that was so bad we were forced to lock ourselves in the small sewing room. The windows all broke in the kitchen and it was a terribly frightening experience for a little boy at the age of three.

I remember sleeping in a small, white bed in my folks' bedroom. I also remember the loud snoring that kept me awake. Having five older brothers and sisters meant that our sleeping quarters were minimal. We all slept upstairs and paired up in bed.

Bad storms were quite an event, and something to be feared. Lightning could strike the house or barn. Whenever we had an electrical storm we all got dressed and sat in the kitchen waiting for the storm to pass by.

I remember all the emphasis in my family on the spiritual part of life. Before going to bed at night, we got on our knees by the bed and said our prayers. My parents set that example. We understood the importance of it and so we followed that example. Praise God for dedicated and devoted parents.

The home of Martin E. and Nellie Nienhuis on the corner of 124th Avenue and Tyler Street in Olive Township, which the family referred to as the "homestead."

I began school in 1921. My first days at school were quite an experience, as the teacher was very disciplinary. He couldn't really teach unless he could control the students, and the more he tried to control them, the more they challenged him. It was all so rigid, as I remember; as a little five-year-old boy, it all looked so dangerous. The older pupils were not of the best behavior and along with that came punishment. In the winter, it was necessary for the teacher to go to the basement and fire up the furnace, and the pupils would become very unruly, including jumping up to walk on the desks, which looked very bad to me. One time he came back a little sooner than expected and there were serious consequences. I can remember seeing the teacher hit and slap the perpetrator until there were yells for mercy.

For me, it was such a frightening experience that I was afraid to say a word in class. I was worried I would say the wrong thing and be punished, and this became a real issue. Sooner or later, something had to be done. I remember my father coming past the school with horses and wagon, as he did quite often on his way from our farm to another piece of property we owned. This time he stopped, and I was right there and remember the teacher telling my father that I wouldn't talk in class. After that, the teacher helped me speak my first word in class. He put a dime on the page of the book I was to read, and asked me what it was. I told him, "It's a dime," and that was the beginning of my learning and talking. Now I can say that I had to be paid to say my first word (I kept the dime).

School was a whole lot better after that. We had this same teacher seven or eight years, and I experienced many strict directions before I graduated from the eighth grade. I can only say "thank you" now. I sure learned right from wrong and respect for my elders. I felt well prepared for high school.

The school bell was rung just once, and if we were not in school when the door was closed we were subject to discipline. We'd either have to stay after school or stay in at recess time. During school hours, we could hear the clock tick. We never raised our hands if we had a question; instead, we raised our book covers. We never had report cards in those days. Our records were in the teacher's big green book. Whenever the drawer wasn't locked and the teacher wasn't around, we would look up our marks. One of the most exciting things I can remember happening at school was when I was in the small room, second or third grade, and my brother Bill opened our door and said, "The school is on fire!" We hurried out, and not in the most orderly way but rather only with what we could grab, and stood outside and watched the school burn. None of us felt too bad about that.

We went a couple weeks without school, and then an old house was fixed up as a new school for us. It was just so nice to go there. We spent about five months in that old house, and the walk was only about half as far for me, so I could run all the way. The burning of the old school was due to an overheated furnace or a bad chimney, so having school in that old house worked out real well, and the next fall we went to a nice new school.

It was great going to the new school. It had a small room and a big room; grades one, two, three and four were in the small room. But the new school was different, as us younger ones had a lady teacher, so we weren't subject to the strict discipline of the man teacher.

The Importance of Church

I will say this: South Olive Christian Reformed Church has meant a lot to me throughout the many years that I have been privileged to live.

I remember going to church with the horse and buggy. Many people at that time had surreys, which were two-seated buggies and could hold six or more people. The church barns were there to put the horses in while we attended services.

DEDICATION

of the

MICHIGAN STATE
HISTORICAL MARKER

for the historic

SOUTH OLIVE
CHRISTIAN REFORMED CHURCH

SOUTH OLIVE
CHRISTIAN REFORMED CHURCH
Sunday, June 30, 1985

I remember the many things that were said about Reverend Jacob Wyngaarden, who was minister at South Olive before I was born.[4] Reverend James Bruinooge[5] is the minister that baptized me and he impressed me with his forceful preaching. Many times, when we as kids used to play church, I would try to preach like him. I never fully understood him because it was all in Dutch, but I loved the influential style of his preaching, his voice going up and down.

I do remember home visitation with Rev. Bruinooge, and shaking hands with that man made such an impression on me. I made the mistake of giving him my left hand and my dad corrected me. I felt so cheap.

We had catechism on Saturday mornings and the pastor taught all of us. I remember the question he always asked us all first, before we prayed: "Marvin Nelson" – or whomever he chose – "How do we pray?" The answer was: close your eyes, fold your hands, and sit up straight.

A lot of strange things used to happen in church: for instance, the way people seated themselves in the pews. In those first years when I was real small, my folks always sat together, but lots of other couples and families like Grandma and Grandpa Nienhuis and the people their age sat separate from one another until their dying day. Families would split up: women on the right as you enter, men on the left. Boys sat with their dad, and girls with their mother. Perhaps not to mix the sexes.

There were morning and afternoon services. No electricity was available in those early days, so services were by lantern and candle if it got dark. I remember the members deciding to invest in a Delco electric system for our church. This was an added responsibility for the pastor, to crank up the motor and see to it that it was running so we could have a meeting at night. For some reason or other, those night sermons were in English instead of Dutch. What a thrill, to go to church and listen and understand God's word being preached! Sometimes the lights would go out when there was Delco motor trouble in the basement of the parsonage.

Usually candles and lamps were available while the motor problems would be corrected[6] and the sermon would continue.

I remember when I first started going to church and all the boredom we endured. All of us kids would sit by Dad, and if we did anything unusual that might be a distraction to anyone else, that strong hand would come down and there would be a pinch hurtful enough to be remembered to this day.

In those days, when boys got to be men they didn't sit with their parents. They sat in the back of church. Why this was, I don't know, but it was an expected thing. It was considered a grown-up thing to do, but some of these young men weren't on their best behavior. Occasionally, the pastor would have to stop preaching because something annoyed him. The entire congregation knew when something was wrong: it would be so quiet we could hear a pin drop. I can remember one pastor who stopped and waited quite a while and then he remarked, "All right fellows, you had your turn. Now it's mine."

For a couple services, the sun was flashing in the pastor's face. Somebody with a mirror was catching the sun's rays and flashing them at the pastor. The situation got so bad that the consistory decided to put somebody in the back of church to watch who was misbehaving. That action created more problems than it was worth: my Uncle Will[7] was appointed and the young men back there made a mockery of that and him. He reported it to the parents and they could not believe their sons would do such things, so there were some families that left and never returned. My uncle was nicknamed the "sheriff." It solved the problem, but I failed to see the mission emphasis in that remedy.

Our church attendance in those days was very good. In the early 1900s, we had Dutch services, mostly due to the fact that most everybody spoke Dutch. I especially enjoyed the Dutch Psalms, as I loved to sing them as a small boy. I remember an old gentleman who would sing the musical notes to the hymns instead of the words, which didn't make much sense to people who didn't know music.

17

Sunday School was held right after the two o'clock service on Sunday afternoons. That was the service that was changed to English. The Sunday School classes were held in the church auditorium and even though they were separated by age groups it was a mumble jumble in there. Each individual class, however, could hear their teacher.

Our church building was separate from the smaller chapel, which was south of the church. It was quite an interesting thing to watch the pastor in his swallow-tailed suit lead the consistory out of the chapel, down the sidewalk, and up the steps in front of the church. They'd walk down the middle aisle, over the big floor register for the heater in the middle of the church, and to the front where the pastor took his position in front of the podium. He would stop to pray while the elders and deacons found their way to their respective seats up front, along the north side.

The sermons were usually an hour and half and sometimes longer. We had no printed paper bulletins in those days, and announcements got to be quite long. And they were usually right before a long prayer. During that long and usually very orderly prayer, some people fell asleep, which was quite noticeable because of their snoring. Disgusting as it was to hear their loud snores, it sometimes took more than a nudge to wake them up. Sleeping in church was all too common in those days, mainly because the service was in Dutch, and that was a language that so many of us didn't understand. Our presence there didn't seem to have the spiritual significance that it had when the service was in English, and to this day I have a little problem with the fact that they maintained this language barrier for so long. I guess the logic was that at least we were in God's house.

We had a nice pipe organ. The pipes were all in the front of the church; I ought to know, I counted them so many times. When us young fellows were old enough to go to night catechism, we were old enough to pump the church organ. This was quite an important task, so every young man in the church would get his turn. When the organist got up, you got up with them and marched up to the pulpit and entered a door, where there was a long handle in front of you to grab hold of and pump up and down. That filled the bellows with air so that the organist could begin playing. The amount of pumping you had to do depended on who was playing the organ. It wasn't that easy to keep it full of air. The more accomplished the musician, the harder you had to work. If the gauge fell below the mark, then the sound would be affected. When the organist quit, it was time for you to get out and sit on a chair up there on the pulpit. The organist would sit on the other side during the first part of service. While the minister preached, you came down and sat with the congregation.

There are a few things that come to mind with that job: I remember a friend of my brother Bill who had been the victim of a prank. Unrelated to this pumping job, somebody had pulled a chair from under him and he hit his head on the back of the chair and developed sleeping sickness. He would fall asleep at a moment's notice and occasionally it would happen to him on the chair on the pulpit and the minister would have to wake him up.

One fellow who went up to pump the organ decided to jump out the window for a smoke and got back in time for the next song.

You tend to remember the big events that happen, and I remember lots of fires when I was younger. I was about six years old and I was staying home with my mother on a Sunday morning in July. My mother asked if I could smell smoke or see smoke to the east. I looked, and there was a lot of black smoke. Weiner's barn was on fire. Mrs. Weiner was taking care of her little boy, and he was playing with firecrackers in the old straw stack behind the barn. Everything burned except the house while the rest of the family was in church. It so happened on that Sunday that our new pastor, P. D. Van Vliet, was being installed.[8] The Weiner's barn was a terrible loss, but the neighbors got together and before the summer was over another nice hip roof barn was built on their farm and

First cutting of hay, probably Martin on the hayrake and possibly (left to right)
Marvin, Arthur, Willard, Gladys and Ada on the wagon

stands to this day. In those days, people really pulled together and all the work they did was voluntary.

Borculo Christian Reformed Church also burned on another Sunday morning in 1924.[9] The burned shingles went high into the air and burned a couple of barns, also. A nice church was re-built on the spot and it stands there today.

The Olive Center grocery store burned in the winter sometime in the 1920s[10] due to an overheated stove. The family owners moved to California for four years, and the store was never rebuilt. At that time, there was a North Holland Crisp store and the Olive Center store. Those were the good old days when people came to you to do business.

The Harlem Reformed Church burned during World War II[11] and also was rebuilt beautifully.

North Holland Reformed Church burned a bit later,[12] also during World War II, and has also been rebuilt into a beautiful sanctuary, replacing the old wood structure. So all things work out for good, however bad it may seem at the time.

I remember President Harding dying when I was a little boy.[13] I found out later that he had made his inaugural address, one-and-a-half hours long, in the pouring rain outside the Capitol building and developed pneumonia and died. Mother told me to be quiet for a certain length of time in respect of his passing, along with everyone else. It made quite an impression on me, that his passing was to be marked by silence. There was much more respect for men in higher office in those days.

My father, Martin, really believed that men in higher office were placed there providentially and deserved all the respect due them. My father had only a seventh-grade education, but his strong will and determination to stand up for what was right, and the common sense he had on most issues, really demanded my utmost admiration.

Ah there were so many manual jobs in those days. Work! Work! Work! That's all we knew; there was no other thing for healthy, able people to do but work, however dull we became, and all of us knew why: church had to be supported. Children had to go to the Christian school to be taught by a teacher that truly loved the Lord. Bills were to be paid. The farm had to paid for. Machinery had to be fixed when even baling wire couldn't do it. My mother often did most of the household chores while the rest of family was doing field work, picking strawberries, pickles, and beans or hoeing corn.

When I was between the age of seven and fourteen, my job in the summertime was always to take care of the cows. We usually had between ten and fifteen cows. I knew them all by name. One part of this job that really stands out in my mind is having to get the cows out of their twenty-acre pasture, which was some thousand feet beyond the back of the barn. After I would herd them out of the pasture, they would have to be chased through a narrow, fenced alley back into the barn. The cows knew it was time to go in when they saw me come, and quite often they would simply head that way, but it wasn't always easy because my father had a bull in the pasture that would breed the cows and that bull was particularly unpredictable.

One afternoon, I think 1926, I had to get those cows from the pasture, and I went after them as usual, only this time the gentleman cow wasn't too cooperative. It stood there, right in front of me. "Wow," I thought, "it seems like he has other ideas." That animal had grown considerably and wasn't about to let a little guy like me interfere with his harem. I grabbed the biggest stick I could find and decided to use a little persuasion, but the bull took one look at me and seemed to say, "I'll take care of that." His head went down and the next thing I knew, I was riding backwards on his head and his head heaved up and I went flying through the air – luckily toward the barbed wire fence. I still can remember sailing through the air; I didn't even have time to pray, but surely my guardian angel took care of me, as I was no match for all that muscle.

Well, being just a kid, I thought I best leave this job for somebody who can make a better impression on that animal. Ah, I thought, my sisters Ada and Gladys are there in the field; they are bigger and stronger than me, maybe they would do my job and I'll gladly pick strawberries instead.

This almost makes me chuckle yet. Neither one of them seemed to be too anxious to go and do that, but my sister Gladys said, "Sure." She was always willing, and of course, she was older then Ada so she took over the responsibility. She would show who was going to be boss there. Gladys went into the pasture carrying a large fence post too heavy for me to handle. It seemed she was thinking, "I'll take care of that bull." Boy, was I proud of her. She went into the pasture and once again there stood the protector of his harem. The bull let out a snort, and I saw the post she was carrying hit the top of bull's head, where it broke, and from where I was, some hundred yards from the fence, I could see her flying through the air after he threw her like he did me. She crawled as fast as she could underneath the fence and my big sister was crying. Ada and I were worried that she might have been hurt. We all went home and reported on our experiences to Mom and Dad.

Wow! How in the world are we going to milk the cows? It was getting late. Dad was home already. "I'll take care of that," he said. Boy, I was very proud of my dad.

I went along with my dad and made sure I stayed on the right side of the fence. He had a spade in his hand and, sure enough, as he walked up there to chase the cows in toward the barn, the bull did the very same thing to him. Only this time it didn't work. My dad laid that spade on his head so hard that it changed his mind and he very obediently went home to the barn with the rest of the cows. The bull was put in his stall and stayed there until it met its doom by the butcher's axe some months later, and got to be meat for our table.

Taking care of cows wasn't all that bad when there was lot of grass. It was always nice to watch them eat if the area was large enough. You would sit along the road in the fence row. One time I was sitting on a snake hill and didn't know it; I felt something move and, sure enough, it was a snake which made me leave my perch in a hurry.

We had a lot of cousins that would stay at our place. As you know, idleness is the devil's workshop; the kids who lived in town didn't know what to do with themselves. So their parents called Uncle Mart or Aunt Nellie. My mother was such a blessed one, she never complained; what a wonderful helpmate she was for my dad. I can remember only one time that they argued and that was about selling a calf that my dad wanted to raise for milking. But she sold the calf because there were some bills that had to be paid.

One of our cousins, Elmer Nienhuis, spent a lot of time at our house as a child because he lost his mother to cancer when she was in her late thirties. The following summer, he developed polio and almost became an invalid. His right leg never grew right and we all sympathized with him. When he got to be older, he wore a brace on that leg and he could get around pretty good that way. He and I spent a lot of time together, because there were quite a few things he just couldn't do. But when it came to taking care of cows he usually helped. One time, in late August when it was terribly dry, he decided to burn an old brush pile. Well, he was one that liked a little excitement, but he got more than he cared for, as Uncle Will's hay field was next to ours. He started a runaway fire that finally burned itself out, but with a whole lot of complaints from the neighborhood and a whole lot more from my dad.

One time in 1926 or '27, I was supposed to get up early and take care of the cows, but it so happened that cousin Chet Schemper stayed overnight, which he did quite often when we were kids. We woke up and had a real pillow fight and we were having so much fun that we disregarded my dad's call to take care of the cows. When I finally got outside, the cows were over a half-mile from home in the neighbor's field. My brothers Art and Bill got them back to where they belonged. I met my dad in the cornfield and to this day I remember the exact spot, because that is where I got my last licking and, if I remember right, I was black and blue for three weeks. My cousin Chet disappeared and I didn't see him again for a couple of weeks. He ran for home as fast as he could. We shared that punishment together and were not too sure we didn't deserve it.

It was at this time we were seeing more airplanes, as there was an air mail route between Grand Rapids and Milwaukee. Because the cargo had to cross over Lake Michigan, they used seaplanes. There were passenger planes, too, sometimes; they held about twelve passengers, including pilot and crew. It was quite an event for us; we always ran out when they came over, as they were so low that we could see the people wave. One morning we heard one coming over at the regular time. My dad was on the second floor in the barn and he started to wonder if the plane was coming down. It sure seemed like it was having motor trouble, and just as it got above our barn about one thousand feet high, it back-fired and the motor quit. The pilot banked to the south and headed for

Postcard of young-looking Martin on a cultivator pulled by a workhorse team, in early years of owning the homestead

a forty-acre field just east of our other farm, which is where we are living now. We could see the boat-bottom of the plane bounce on the ground. He never used his wheels because the plowed field wouldn't allow it. The pilot could see the road coming right at him, which is now Tyler Street, and that is where the plane stopped.

What an attraction that was! We didn't even have school that day. They must have radioed about their trouble, because smaller planes started landing in the fields, all wanting to see their buddies who crashed. It was because of the fine piloting that nobody was hurt. The plane had plowed the biggest furrows I ever saw in Weiner's field: there were gouges three feet deep and twenty feet long, about three or four of them before he finally came to a stop. The airline company had a crew of three who dismantled the plane in order to salvage it. These fellows stayed right here where we are living until the job was done.

Uncle Bill and Aunt Martha Kooyers were living here at that time. The men from the airline were paid well and they really appreciated Aunt Martha's cooking. We wondered how the neighbors would ever fill in those holes in the field where that seaplane bounced up and down on the pontoon underneath. The crash sure drew a lot of people together in a hurry.

As time went on, my brothers and sisters started getting jobs and going out into the world. My older brother Bill[14] managed to get a job at the Kinsella Glass Company or what we just called the glass factory, where they made mirrors for the furniture business and which later became Donnelly. He went to work with Uncle Harry Schemper, who lived near us and took the horse and buggy to work, a ten-mile trip one-way. In the winter, he'd take the kind of smaller sleigh called a cutter. They would leave very early in the morning and come home late at night. Uncle Harry had a good trotting horse which would trot all way up and back. In those days, they had horse barns to rent for a small fee where they could be fed and watered during the day while the men worked.

26

Possibly Ada, El and Martin pitching hay at the homestead

27

We eventually got that new, yellow Nash automobile, a beautiful car. Around that very same time, my oldest brother, El, got work at Buss Machine Works, a company that made famous woodworking machinery and especially planers. Some interesting things happened during the time he worked at Buss, but during the time he worked there, he wasn't twenty-one years old so most of the money he earned was given to the operation of the family household. He worked there for a number of years until he had a machine accident and cut off the ends of two of his fingers. This encouraged him to go to business college and start on a successful business career.

In the lean years directly after World War I, my dad's main emphasis was on farming, but as money got more plentiful and the farming was good, he decided to modernize the barn and house. Gas light was one of the new things added to our place, and we would have our own gas plant right in the basement.

The new lamps burned carbide gas or acetylene, made by putting calcium carbide in water. Our Uncle Allen Kooyers would supply us and others with the carbide, and we'd put that into a limited amount of water in the gas plant or gas generator; as the gas formed it would raise a float to a certain height and would shut off. It all worked automatically, constantly making new gas as it was needed. We had gas lights in the house, barn and all other buildings.

Our coal furnace was only about five feet from the gas plant in the basement. There was always the chance of an explosion or fire, and we didn't pay enough attention to that. The globes in the barn had to be free of cobwebs. It always was the job of us kids to keep them clear and that we did. Another very important thing was to stay away from the basement gas plant with cigarettes and cigars and pipes. At that time, it seemed everybody had a bad habit of smoking. If it wasn't smoking, it was chewing tobacco.

We all looked forward to the general modernization of the barn and the house. We put new cow stanchions in the barn and installed water systems for both the barn and the house. That was appreciated very much; no more pumping water by hand. It was a large project and also expensive. We had a gasoline engine in the basement that was used for both our washing machine and the water pump. It had to be cranked to start and I can still see my dear mother cranking that thing until she was blue in the face. If I got too close to that engine, the punishment would be swift; she kept a wash stick handy from which I preferred to keep my distance. The well was about one hundred feet away from the house, but first the water had to be pumped to an elevated tank in the barn and then piped back into the house. This tank held at least five hundred gallons of water. The first time we tried to fill it after it was put in, it leaked so bad that everything was flooded in the cow stable. We tried everything to stop the leaks.

This whole job was contracted to Gil VerHoeven of Zeeland. My father was not satisfied with the job and made up his mind not to pay for it until it was fixed right. After my dad called them back to the farm a number of times, VerHoeven decided to fix it once and for all by sealing the inside of the tank with tar. I can still see this being done, standing on the top rung of the ladder. I recall thinking, "Now it's going to be fixed. We are going to have running water in the house like people in the city." Well, it stopped the leaks all right, but the water tasted terrible. My dad was just furious. That was it: the job was not going to be paid until that was corrected. Some time passed and it got to be a real issue. I remember this as if it were yesterday.

My dad was plowing in the field with horses and I was holding the end of the lines walking behind him in the furrows, as little kids liked to do in them days. When my dad reached the end of the row, there were two men waiting, the Sheriff and a deputy. If I ever was proud of my dad, it was then. He started laughing and poking fun of the deputy and his gun. That all looked pretty scary to me. "Well," Dad said, "I'll just have to go home with the horses and invite you in the house for a drink and see how you like it."

They had a drink and admitted it had a bad taste. My dad believed that his complaint was justified and payment would be withheld until corrected. Well, I guess they thought otherwise.

That afternoon we got a call from brother El at his job at Buss Machine Co. He said our car had been stolen. So who do you call? The police, of course. The police had the situation well in hand, and we could pick up the car in Grand Haven, providing we paid the bill to VerHoeven. That was the way things were done in those days. I believe we paid some of the bill. Enough to get our car back. All I can remember is drinking from a water pail with a dipper; the water from the tank could be used for washing and the cows didn't mind the taste at all.

My brother El went on to business college; my sister Gladys went to Holland Christian High School and Sister Ada followed quite soon afterwards. They started at the first Christian high school in the Prospect Park area of Holland and then went to the new high school when it was built at the "Y" where River, State and Michigan avenues meet.[15] I remember going to my first basketball game in 1923, when I was either six or seven. I can even remember a few of the players at the time, their names were Van Darpel, Herringa, and Van Fassen, with the legendary Albert Muyskens as coach.[16] Gladys, Ada and brother Bill all graduated from Holland Christian, went to college, and became teachers.

There were Christmas and Easter programs in those days, and a lot of work was put into them by the teachers at school. They were usually well-attended. People appreciated programs, as they were one of the few sources of entertainment. We had no radio, and certainly no T.V. like we have today. We couldn't have such things as pantomime[17] for Christmas or Easter. That was a big no-no. The Christian stories were believed to be too holy for replication.

I remember an Easter program in which I had a very special part: I was just seven years old and dressed in my new blue serge wool suit and big red bow tie, which my mother had made for

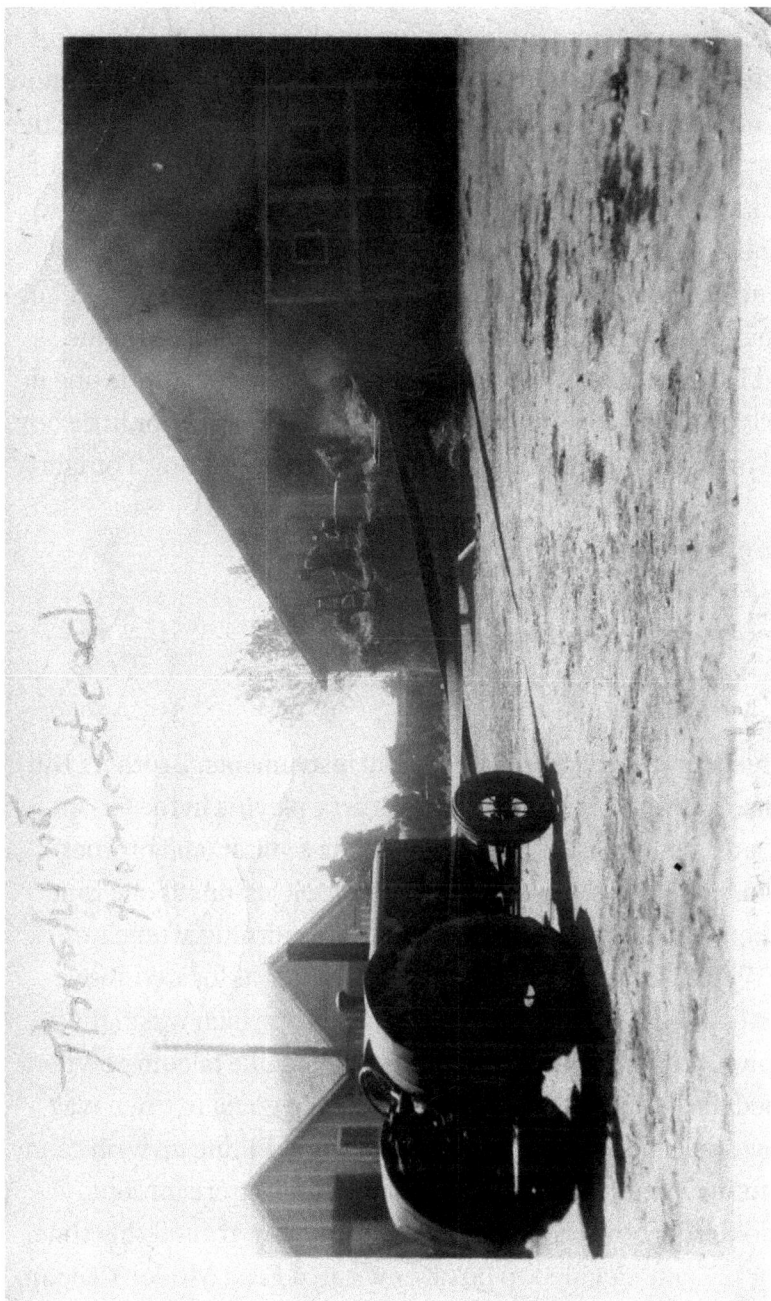

Running a threshing machine off the tractor at the homestead. Look closely off the nose of the tractor and you'll see there's someone bringing in another horse-drawn wagon piled high with grain

me. I sang a song, "Easter Time, Easter Time," in front of some older girls who answered me in the song. I went up in front of the church all by myself and looked down on that whole building full of people and all those white tops and bald heads. Little did I know then that I would be bald most of my life after I grew up. After the program, I received a lot of compliments. It was the beginning of lots of singing for me.

In those days, 1924–25, every district had a school and a lot of Parent Teacher Association, or PTA, meetings were held. They would have special programs in order to get the people to come out, and I sang at a lot of those. One I remember well: it was one in East Crisp School. My aunts were in it and I was the poor little boy dressed in rags who sang "Where is My Wandering Boy Tonight?":

Where is my wandering boy tonight–
The boy of my tenderest care,
The boy that was once my joy and light,
The child of my love and prayer?

After this, my folks decided to get us all instruments. Brothers Bill and El had a saxophone that they took turns playing in the Crisp Band. Later, sister Gladys had a banjo, Ada a guitar, and brother Art had a violin. I had a mandolin. We all took lessons at one time or another. Bill, Art and I went on Saturday morning after catechism. We had lessons with Mr. Babbitt, who was located above Meyer Music House, a music instrument store which was right downtown.[18] I remember Mr. Babbitt smelled like talcum powder. It seemed like he bathed in it. The best part of going to town was spending some money at a five and dime store. Filling up with candy, chocolate-covered peanuts and occasionally an ice cream cone.

My oldest brother El was making big money around this time, 1926 or '27, and decided to buy a new car, a Ford Model T sedan. He brought it home when my cousin Chet Schemper happened to be at our house playing with me. We had such a good time that afternoon. We found a nest of rotten eggs behind the barn and got such a kick out of hearing them pop as we threw them against the walls of the big building. Just then, El was asked to take our neighbor Mrs. Looman[19] home, and we could go along in his brand new car. We got into the back seat and it wasn't long before we were ordered out with a big, "Pew! You kids stink!"

Brother Bill had a little difficulty learning how to drive. One time he went into the garage to back out the Old 1918 Nash. He started it up without any problem, but instead of putting it in reverse he put it in low. A top buggy was parked inside the garage in front of the car, because we still used it once in a while. Well, that top buggy went right on ahead of the car straight through the back of the garage and up into the hay mow. The Nash had a dent cut into the fender the exact size of the buggy wheel, and it remained there as long as we had the car; we drove that car until about 1928, about three years after the occasion of this mishap.

Brother Bill was learning to drive when he came up to the tracks of the interurban line, a trolley train between Holland and Zeeland which ran along the route of what was later called M21. I was riding in the back of the 1918 Nash, and I remember him slamming on the brakes to avoid a collision. Quite soon after that incident I remember the trolley was shut down. Brother El was his instructor and really complimented Bill on his awareness. I can still see them taking the tracks out and laying the ground work for the new highway between Holland and Zeeland. Cars were becoming more plentiful so that was called M21 or Old M21 as it is today.

We furnished the Holland Rusk Company with milk at that time, where they used it to make the crisp, twice-baked biscuits. We usually took six ten-gallon metal cans of milk a day, five days a week. We took the seats out of the back of the Nash and the six cans just fit in the back. Bill would take the milk to the rusk factory and then go on to school at Holland Christian. Ada and he rode together until they graduated. My dad was determined to have us all go to Holland Christian. Gladys had already graduated from there and went on to Hope College, as did Ada later on. Both got their teaching certificate and taught in the Holland area close to home.

Brother Bill also did very well in high school, but he suffered some ill effects from a diptheria vaccination and almost died. After he got the shot, he went into convulsions and the doctor believed the reaction to be something out of the ordinary. He didn't expect him to live. He got well, but he was never the same. He went on to college and got his teaching certificate as well, and also taught in the neighborhood, but he developed serious problems while teaching. He made many strange decisions. His troubles were so hard for our parents to accept, as he was such a good student. He taught all eight grades and managed to get through that first year. But his fiancée gave him the gate, ending their courtship, which didn't help. At that time, my brother Arthur shared his concerns with me that he believed brother Bill was losing it. The family came to the conclusion that the diptheria shot he had received had done permanent damage. From that time on, not one of us was ever permitted to have a vaccination of any kind, Dad and Mom's orders.

After Bill graduated, my dad got rid of the Nash and he bought a 1928 Chevy roadster that could be used as a four-seater coupe, a two-seater roadster, or as a pickup truck. Was that ever nice! We would put a truck box on it and haul our six cans of milk to the rusk factory and whenever we went out for dates we could remove the box and put in the rumble seat. Well, it wasn't long after that we decided to buy a big 1927 Buick that would hold the whole family and then some. Was that ever a swell car in those days. It was a sedan with real glass windows; no more side curtains. What a car.

El had a close call driving that 1928 Chevy roadster. It was around 1930 that El and his girlfriend and later his wife, Henrietta Dekker, went out for a picnic lunch with sister Ada and her boyfriend in the Pottawattomie Bayou area of the Grand River.[20] On the way home, they failed to stop at the intersection of 120th Ave and M50,[21] and they were hit broadside by a DeVaux[22] car driven by a Grand Rapids man and family. The 1928 Chevy that El and his passengers were riding in rolled over three times and landed in the ditch right side up. Some people riding in the other car were seriously hurt, but El and the others came out of it pretty good, just bumps and bruises.

El was in the wrong, but he had insurance. He had to rely on them to pay the bills. Well, then he found out the insurance company, Triple A, had gone bankrupt,[23] which so many other companies were doing in the Depression. So the only thing my brother could do is go bankrupt also. Once again, he had to start over. My mother felt so bad about it; she cried over his wrecked car which stood in the yard for some time before it was hauled away.

At this time, my brother El went into the milk business with another fellow; they had a milk route in Zeeland. He was given some bad guidance and was steered into a poor business deal. Just when they went into business, the City of Zeeland decided they did not want outsiders delivering milk in the city, and so brother El lost out. It was a tough blow for him, but he decided to go into the grocery business. With his business college education, he accepted a job as manager of a Kroger store in Zeeland. Then he was transferred to a store in Battle Creek and then, after a couple years, he came to Holland and managed a store in the vicinity of Holland Christian High School, where I was going at the time. He was very successful at this and later had his own IGA store, which he operated until supermarkets took over and ran him out of business.

At the homestead with (left to right) Martin, Marlan, Nellie and Roger

PART II

"Rugged Individuals" – the Nienhuis and Kooyers Families

The Nienhuis Family

I remember both my Grandma Emma and Grandpa Eildert Nienhuis. My grandfather Eildert M. Nienhuis came to this country from the Netherlands with his father Martinus Nienhuis and mother Atje in 1854. My Grandma Emma (née Workman)[24] came to this country along with her brothers as orphans. Their trip across the ocean took over thirty days. The picture on the wall at Grandma and Grandpa's farmhouse in North Holland showed the ship that she came to this country on. When we went to Grandma's house that picture really impressed me.

Grandpa Eildert Nienhuis was born in the Netherlands[25] and was only four or five years old when he arrived in the U.S., along with his three brothers and one sister.[26] My great-grandparents, Martinus and Atje, were farmers in North Holland. Great-grandma Atje died at fifty-four years old in North Holland in 1870. My great-grandfather, Martinus, died in North Holland in 1890 at the age of seventy.[27]

Grandma Emma's brothers settled in Chicago. I remember very well taking trips to Chicago to see the Workman relatives. My parents would first take Grandma Emma over there in the old 1918 Nash, and brother El would drive in those days. It took the whole day to get there. Occasionally, we would get postcards back at the farm sent to us from Benton Harbor, which was one of the many stops along the way.

So many of these Workman relatives are still living in Chicago today. I spent a lot of time visiting in Chicago as a kid. It was a thrill to be in the big city, and I remember riding the elevated trolley and visiting the Field Museum of Natural History and Buckingham Fountain and the Museum of Science and Industry and the big stores with escalators with some very precious relations.[28]

I remember my grandfather Eildert being sick and dying of cancer in 1921. He was seventy-one years old when he died.[29] He was laid on his bed and all dressed up in his best clothes. In those days, most things like funeral preparations were taken care of by the family. His black hair and beard never grayed at all. I was five years old at the time, and it made quite an impression on me.

Grandma Emma died thirty years later at the age of eighty-seven or eighty-eight. We're not sure how old she was, exactly, because we didn't know her birthday.[30] She had rooms attached to Uncle Abel and Aunt Hattie's house, but for quite a while toward the end of her life she was taken care of by my parents at their home on the corner of 124th and Tyler. This was at the same time that my wife Dorothy and I were also living there. During the first four years of our marriage, we lived at home with my parents and Dot got a lot of calls during the night to help Grandma. I can still hear her call for help by hitting the floor with a broom next to her bed and calling to Dorothy. My dear wife was very much appreciated as she waited on her night and day for about a month. Grandma did go back to her home as her condition worsened and she died there.

The Kooyers Family

My mother Nellie's maiden name was Kooyers and I was very involved with their family, too. Grandma and Grandpa Kooyers were married in June 1882. Grandma's name was Geertye Meengs, and she was born Oct 5, 1861, and died Jan 28, 1925. Grandpa Berend Wilham Kooyers (called William) was born July 27, 1865, and died Nov 22, 1940.[31]

It seems my childhood memories are more clear on experiences at the Kooyers Farm than the Nienhuis farm, mainly because there were more attractions. My mother's family consisted of six girls and three boys living, so she had five younger sisters and three younger brothers. I understand my grandmother had thirteen children in all, some of whom died in infancy of diptheria and scarlet fever. There was always so much more going on at their house.

As a child, I remember all the trips to Grandma and Grandpa Kooyers', especially for Thanksgiving and Christmas. Sometimes my mother and I would walk the two miles to their home. It was easy walking over there, but very tiresome walking home because of playing all day. The holidays were always spent at Grandma and Grandpa's. In those days, the Fourth of July was a very special day, and fireworks were cheap and plentiful. We had homemade ice cream if we couldn't afford store-bought ice cream.

Theirs was a large farm and my grandfather was known to be quite well to do. He had his brother Aldert, a bachelor, running the farm while he was on the road selling and bargaining. Grandpa Kooyers' farm operation was at an all-time high at the turn of the century.

His place had a store which also served as a post office, so there were many people coming and going there. My mother, being the oldest in the family, related many of her experiences with us as a young girl. I remember this one especially:

She was only nine years old when they seemed to be missing stuff not only in the store but also in the basement of the home.[32]

This seemed to be happening more frequently as days passed. The family made their own cheese and butter, and certain things that were kept in the cellar for preservation were missing. Then the store was also broken into and it got to be a big issue.

It seems those things weren't handled by the law as well as they should have been, and it got to be a matter of taking things into your own hands.

My grandfather took care of the business, so he was gone a lot; quite often he would leave home for a trip and come home the next day. He and his brother Aldert were rugged individuals. My grandpa advised his hired man, DeVries, who took care of the store, to just take the shotgun and lay for the intruder. DeVries agreed and found a place in back of the store where he could hide. He locked the door and waited inside to see who might show up. It happened to be a moonlit night.

The intruder found the door locked. He was determined to get in. He left and came back later. Shortly after midnight, the hired man heard something again at the door. He raised his 12-gauge shotgun and aimed at the door. There was a long wait: the thief was determined to get into the store, and it took an hour or more for him to drill the lock out of the door. In the process, he would look into the window and it was a nerve-racking experience for the hired man, DeVries. He stood in a leveled-off position all the time it took him to drill out the lock, and he stood motionless because there was just enough moonlight for him to be seen. He didn't know whether or not the robber had a gun. Finally, the door opened and the person walked in the door, where he was shot point blank in the chest. He turned around and walked a bit and then fell and crawled to the straw stack near the barn. The hand tracks in the sand showed the anguish he went through. They covered him with a blanket and the body laid there until the police arrived from Grand Haven at twelve o'clock noon the next day.

It was shocking to find out that it was the neighbor boy, Dyk was his last name, who had had quite a conversation with my grandfather just the day before. My grandfather had been on his way to Grand Haven with a load of hay when he stopped to pick up a rider. Quite often people did that in those days, but this rider was quite an inquisitive fellow, wanted to know the lay of the land. In those days, neighbors always had the time or took the time to visit, regardless of how busy they were. It was shocking for him to find out later that it was the same young man that was shot on his premises that night.

My mother, who was nine years old at the time, remembered the hired man, DeVries, coming into the house after he shot him. He turned all the chairs upside down; he was completely beside himself. I really don't know all the details as to how these things were handled in those days, but I do know that Mr. DeVries was cleared because it was a case of self-defense.

Grandmother Gertie Kooyers, who had nine living children and four still-born,[33] suddenly took sick with pneumonia and passed away in 1924.[34] She died at home, as very seldom people went to the hospital. It was wintertime, so I rode on the sleigh with Mom and Dad. My Uncle Allen Kooyers was the only one home at the time and he asked my folks and me if we wanted to see her, and we went into the room off the kitchen and there she laid on a stretcher (as they called it in those days), cold and still. It all looked so gruc-some to a little six-year-old.[35]

The folks decided that I should not go to the funeral, because I had whooping cough, so I stayed right here in the house on Tyler Street where we now live, with people who were living here at the time. I remember playing outside with my little sled that I got for Christmas, and I just stood and watched the funeral procession go down the main road: first the funeral caisson and then relatives and friends on horse-drawn sleighs. What a sad day for a little guy.

My Grandpa William had a hard time accepting Grandma Gertie's death. He was suffering reverses on the farm. Cattle were dying very mysteriously, and he also made some poor investments.

Difficulties were adding up. Instead of trusting in the Lord, he went elsewhere. An uncle and aunt in our family were involved with spiritualists at meetings in Grand Rapids[36]; they influenced Granddad to come to the meetings with them. They had all the answers. They told him why all the cattle had died. If he wanted to know anything, these spiritualists could tell him. Grandpa and others reached the point where they became very satisfied with the information they received there. If anything was lost, they had to ask the spiritualists. He was so influenced by their meetings or séances that he even believed they could talk to the dead.

My grandpa was told by the spiritualists that he could talk to my grandma at the stroke of midnight if he would listen for the pump handle to rattle. He was to get up and go into the kitchen in his house and Grandma would be there to talk to him. So he listened for the rattle and sure enough it happened. His words were answered in Dutch. I was staying at the house and I was scared, so I pulled the blanket over my head and stayed in bed. Then we, as kids, heard these things; we and all the rest of my cousins got a big kick out of that. Most of us had a lot of questions we wanted answered, but that was for certain people who believed in fortune telling and that was of the devil. Our parents set us straight on that.

My uncle the spiritualist got to be a divine healer, and because of that influence the relationship between uncles and aunts became very seriously strained.

The Church became involved and many meetings were held. We, as kids, did not know at that time how serious it all was until we heard that Grandma Kooyers had been poisoned and that was the reason for her death.[37] The entire large family of uncles and aunts was bitterly divided on the issue, and the dispute would soon become much worse. There seemed to be some truth in thinking about poison, as a number of cattle had died for some unknown reason at the time and an investigation found arsenic and powdered glass in the cattle feed.[38] This created great suspicion, and through

42

the influence of the satanic people in Grand Rapids who were associated with my uncle and aunt,[39] that brought the blame down on Uncle Bill and Aunt Martha Kooyers, who were living with Grandma and Grandpa at the time.[40] Aunt Martha did the house-work while Uncle Bill worked full time on the farm with his two brothers, Allen and Raymond, and his Uncle Aldert, my grandpa's brother who never married.

Because she was there every day in the house, and looked after my grandma, my Aunt Martha was suspected of poisoning her. Some members of the family and the community believed this, and many did not. The family situation went from bad to worse. It was heartbreaking for Aunt Martha and Uncle Bill, and it got to be impossible for them to live on the farm under those circumstances. But the times were difficult; Depression days were setting in.

My grandfather was a big farmer and well to do until he became involved in all these satanic rituals. It took a lot of money to get the information he needed from the spiritualists, to find all the answers to his questions, and they also influenced him to invest in phony stock. The "thick neck people," as he called them in Dutch.[41]

It was a sad state of affairs. Grandma was not there to steer Grandpa in the right direction.

My mother was the oldest child in that Kooyers family and she did not believe the accusations against Uncle Bill and Aunt Martha. The situation got so bad that my father finally decided to fix up our other farm home, the house on Tyler Street where we live now, and told Uncle Bill and Aunt Martha that they could live there. So at least they were out of that suspicious environment. But the false accusations didn't stop there.

The bad blood was festering and the family decided to solve the problem once and for all: Grandma's body would have to be exhumed and tested for evidence of poisoning. So after a lot of planning and contacts with Lansing medical examiners, they went ahead and opened the grave and opened the coffin and found that nothing had changed. Investigators removed a small part of her

Third Annual Reunion

—OF—

NIENHUIS FAMILY

Labor Day, 1930

—AT—

Lone Oak Park

Pres., Martin E. Nienhuis

Sec., A. A. Nienhuis

Treas., Albert A. J. Nienhuis

Chr. Program Com.,
A. J. Nienhuis

Chr. Sport Com.,
J. N. Nienhuis

We'll Work Till Jesus Comes

O land of rest, for thee I sigh,
  When will the moment come,
When I shall lay my armor by,
  And dwell in peace at home?

Chorus—
  We'll work till Jesus comes,
  We'll work till Jesus comes,
  We'll work till Jesus comes,
  And we'll be gathered home.

No tranquil joys on earth I know,
  No peaceful sheltering dome;
This world's a wilderness of woe,
  This world is not my home.

I sought at once my Saviour's side,
  No more my steps shall roam;
With Him I'll brave death's chilling tide,
  And reach my heav'nly home.

44

PROGRAM

12 O'clock

Meeting called to order by Pres. M. E. Nienhuis

Invocation by Jacob Braak

DINNER HOUR

Remarks by the President

Singing—"Star Spangled Banner"
Ada Nienhuis, Pianist

Talk by Elder M. Nienhuis

Instrumental Duet—
Ethel and Johanna Nienhuis

Recitation by Priscilla Nienhuis

Letter from Jean Nienhuis in China—
Read by J. Brinkman

PLAY

SLAVE GIRL AND SCHOOL GIRL
Directed by Henrietta Brinkman

Mr. Ding, a book seller—Peter Nienhuis
Mrs. Ding, his wife—Evelyn Knoll
Kou-Ying, his daughter—Ethel Redder
Mr. Siong Lo, a neighbor—Paul Brinkman
Ya-T'ou, a slave girl—Mrs. Bertha Nienhuis
Miss Simmons, a teacher in a Mission School—
Berdina Vinkemulder

Hymn: "We'll work till Jesus comes" (By request
of Jean Nienhuis)—see last page.

Music by Orchestra—
Charles Van Dornink
Martin Reindert
Willard Nienhuis
David Van Vliet
Ada Nienhuis

Reading—David Van Vliet
Song—Marvin Nelson Nienhuis
Family History—A. A. Nienhuis
Music—Orchestra (Collection)
Psalm Singing—Nienhuis Octett
Psalm 134 in unison.

liver and tested it for poisons, but found nothing, which was definite proof that she died a natural death, and that took care of all that nonsense.

But from that time on, nothing was right again at Grandpa's. Relationships between uncles and aunts were never the same. Uncle Aldert, Grandpa's brother who had been running the farm, was invited to live with his sister, as there was nothing left on the Kooyers farm that he could call his own. He never married and lived with his sister, Mrs. Kiekover,[42] until he died.

Uncle Allen and my granddad got into a serious argument which turned into a fist fight. If it hadn't been for a neighbor interfering, they would have killed each other. Uncle Allen left and didn't return for a long time and nobody knew where he was. He managed to get a good job at General Motors in Flint. We all were so happy about that. He met a real nice Hungarian gal and was happily married. About ten years after that, he bought a farm and had some good years in the Flint area.

Uncle Raymond was born when my Grandma was over fifty years old, so he was the trailer of that family, born eight years after Allen. So many of his nephews were twice his age and had to call him uncle. But we always felt sorry for him after Grandma died.

When Uncle Ray was a small boy, I was told he had trouble in school. He was only five years older than me. At that time, if kids stayed home not much was said about it. That is something his parents didn't seem to know and it could be that he didn't want them to know. So Grandpa and Grandma would make his lunch and he would say his good bye and they figured he went to school. The teacher, meanwhile, figured he stayed home, but they were a little careful about discussing these absences in those days because there were no child labor laws. This went on for six weeks. Uncle Raymond wasn't at home or at school. Where did Uncle Raymond go?

There was an old discarded top buggy – a horse-drawn buggy with a top on it – sitting in the woods, and that's where he spent six weeks just to stay out of school. Eventually, he did get a good education and turned out to be quite a capable and able man, but he sure had a lonesome life with Grandpa until he became old enough to work. When he was old enough, he went to work with Uncle Bill at the Limbert Company in Holland, where they made high-quality Arts and Crafts furniture. That's where he met Aunt Ellen Coffey and was happily married soon thereafter[43] and had a nice family.

My grandfather Kooyers lived by himself quite a few years on the farm.[44] He had a wire baler and he would hire himself out with that; he went to almost every farm around to bale hay and straw. This kept him busy most of the time in the summers. His lifestyle was far from good. Vagabond-ish, I would say. Quite often he would stop in at our house on 124th after one of his long journeys on foot to Grand Haven, a trip of at least ten miles one-way.[45] He didn't seem to acknowledge how much he'd lost. He always seemed to be on top of everything, never down. I would say he was always welcomed in our house, but my dad let him know what he thought of his lifestyle and the trouble he'd brought on himself.

My mom and her sisters – Grandpa's daughters – would always make a point of cleaning the house for Grandpa every Friday. There was a parlor in that house that we had seldom seen. It had beautiful plush furniture in it, and a nice spinning wheel which Grandma had used earlier in their lives. There were antiques of all kinds, including a beautiful cuckoo clock. I'd watched him pull the weights to wind that clock many a time.

He took in boarders in the house. One couple stayed with him for a while, but the arrangement was all but good. The woman had a bad reputation and they stayed there until they got sick and died. After this experience, my grandfather decided one summer to rent the house to some Mexican migrants. He cleared out of the house and made a place for himself in the barn, but what happened was the worst. Either a careless fire in the fireplace or stove or smoking caused the house to catch fire and it burned to the ground. It was a tragedy that all those precious antiques, pictures and keepsakes had all gone up in smoke. I can still see my aunts crying their eyes out over it. That was definitely the end of the house cleaning, at least at that house.

Grandpa continued living in the barn, whenever he wasn't staying by my aunt and uncle the divine healers in Holland. It was on a Sunday evening that we were aroused by our party line phone ringing, which meant trouble. We looked to the east and the sky was red. We hurried over to the Kooyers farm to see the last of the large, 120-foot-long barn burn. Apparently, Grandpa was moving some hay while doing the chores with a kerosene lantern and the hay caught fire. Everything burned to the ground and that was the end of Grandma and Grandpa's place. That proves what can happen when the devil has its way. Everything was gone. The origin of the fire was investigated, but soon the matter was dropped.

From that time on, Granddad had to go it alone. His lifestyle was pitiful. He really wasn't the kind of person that anyone would care to have around, unless it was for mercy's sake. He was a talkative person, and when he spoke he expected you to listen; if not, he would shake you and make you listen. How often he would say to me in Dutch terrible words and cursing (you know them but you don't dare to say it). He always spoke Dutch to the adults; he didn't like to speak English, although he could. Maybe he didn't want us kids to hear some of the terrible things he was saying.

It wasn't long after he moved to Holland that he became ill with dropsy,[46] and this was more than my aunt could handle. The divine healer just couldn't come up with the right remedy.

In 1938, with all the love my own mother had for her good father, which he once was, she and my dad decided to take care of him. She often said to us: "Remember, Grandpa wasn't always like this." So, he moved in with us: it was Dad, Mom, me, my two younger brothers Cliff and Rog, and Grandpa. Never too much for my dear mother. Praise the Lord! What love. Grandpa lingered for some time. I remember Dr. VandenBerg sharing some of his experiences with Grandpa with me. He did all he could do to relieve his suffering: Grandpa was tapped again and again to remove the water build-up which made him so terribly uncomfortable. The doctor remarked about Grandpa's incredible tolerance for pain. He was an unbelievably rugged individual.

Grandpa always enjoyed it when my dad read the Bible to him. He found comfort in that, as I recall. I'm sure he had a lot of time to think while he was ill and God only knows how some of these things turn out, but during the last days of his life, all his wrongs seemed to confront him. He couldn't correct them, but I'm sure he found the peace that passes understanding. He died peacefully at our home with all of us there in 1940. I remember that the family had to buy a suit for him to be buried in, and paid for the funeral.

4th July 1938 Manistee

Bub and Dot on the beach in Manistee, July 4, 1938

50

PART III

The Flying Challenger from Crisp

My older brother Arthur had one year in at Holland Christian High School in 1932, when he took over the job of delivering the milk, as Bill had graduated. Art wore a coverall over his school clothes while he made his delivery, and then he left it in the rusk factory and went on to school. I had just graduated from the eighth grade and stayed at home to help on the farm for the first semester, and then I became a half-year student at Holland Christian High School on the first of February. Boy, what an experience that was, going from an eight-grade country school to a big city school. Having that many students in one class was hard to get used to. It was all so strange, having a different teacher for every subject, but I soon got used to the arrangement.

Art and I had it made, and everything was going well until Art got sick with the flu on Washington's birthday, February 22. We drove the milk to the rusk factory and we took the milk in, and when it was time for Art to go take off his coverall, he sat on the steps and remarked to me that he wasn't going to high school that day. I wasn't feeling all that great either, so we decided to go home. Little did I know that this was going to be our last trip home together.

Art and I shared a bed, so we talked to one another. He believed he had the flu, but that night he asked me to feel his stomach and there was a hard lump there. He asked me not to mention it, for fear that he might have to go to the hospital. Well, the next day I went to high school and stayed in town by the house of Henrietta Dekker, my older brother El's girlfriend, for the rest of the week.

When I got home on Friday things were looking somewhat better. The doctor came a couple of times and believed that he had some kind of infection due to the flu.

On Sunday afternoon, we went to church and Dad and Mother stayed home with Art. They were worried. It was at this time that something terrible happened: all of a sudden, he yelled of unbearable pain.

Uncle Bill and Aunt Martha were coming to see him, and as they approached our place on foot they could hear him yell. In those days, we usually walked anywhere close in the neighborhood. At this time, Uncle Bill and Aunt Martha were considered part of the family. During the Depression, they lived on our other farm[47] and they did the chores for rent. Uncle Bill was a hired hand on our farm.

When Art yelled out, the doctor was called and he still believed it was just a result of the flu. He believed Art would start vomiting and that this would relieve him somewhat, and that is what he did. It was brown, the way the doctor said. It turned out to be the worst night he ever lived and one I will never forget. The folks were up with him at his bedside all night. Of course, I tried to sleep in another room next to his. The dimly lit lantern stood in the hall as it usually did, as we all slept upstairs. It was a night that none of us slept well.

I could hear my father reading by the dim kerosene lantern and discussing the Bible with Art. I faintly remember that he read from Psalms. Arthur had plans of becoming a confessing member and was concerned about his salvation. I could hear him praying for God to be merciful to him, a sinner. As I heard this, I thought he was delirious because of the fever he had developed. It was a long night, and in the morning I asked him what I should tell his friends at school and his remark was: "Tell them I'm never coming back." I still didn't realize the seriousness of his illness. I kidded with him and went along to town with Uncle Harry[48], who hauled the milk for him at that time.

The doctor was called again in the morning and he immediately remarked to my dad that Art was dying. They gave him something intravenously and rushed him to the hospital. Uncle Harry Schemper carried him downstairs and placed him in between Mom and Dad on the back seat of our Buick.

At noon that same day, my sister Ada came running up the Holland High School steps to tell me that they had taken Art to the hospital and I should go with her right away.

As Art rode to the hospital, he complained about it getting dark and being so hot. He finally got to the hospital where he should have gone much earlier. Now he remarked to Mother that he would get some sleep. He had had so many sleepless nights. Mother mentioned the fact to him that she didn't think he would get well again. His reply was, "That's alright, too."

It was shortly after, while sister Ada and I were sitting in the waiting room at the hospital, that I heard my dad running down the hospital stairs to tell us if we wanted to see Arthur alive we should come quickly. I can truthfully say that was the greatest shock of my life. I tried to talk to Art, but he couldn't answer. Yes, God took him. It was over. I remember seeing the doctor check his pulse and say to Dad, "Why didn't you take him in here before?" This happened right after the doctor had a consultation. What our doctor had thought was just the flu was something much more serious. It was explained that it was probably a quick cancer or a peptic ulcer or a ruptured appendix, to this day we really don't know.[19]

Mother was devastated. What a sad feeling as we rode home from the hospital on a nice, bright, sun-shiny afternoon on Leap Year Twenty-Ninth of February, 1932. Art was eighteen years old. My dad held up well; being by Art's bedside the night before and hearing his wonderful commitment to Jesus surely was a real comfort to him and us all. That's why he said it was alright if God willed it otherwise. The Holy Spirit spoke and comforted.

How we missed him at first, coming home amidst all the crying and tears. Going down in the basement to put on our barn clothes and seeing his clothes hanging right where he put them is something I'll never forget.

53

Arrangements were made with Langeland funeral home. It was the next day when we saw the hearse arrive at noon. The whole family was home. The coffin was moved into the master bedroom, where he laid in state for two days before the funeral. Our suits had crepes sewed on the one arm and the girls wore black for one year, as it was in those days.

The funeral was held at South Olive Christian Reformed Church. All the neighbors got together to help plan the funeral and offered help in any way they could. Many friends and neighbors and relatives came to visit the body at our house. On the funeral day, services were held at one o'clock at our house and two o'clock at the church. The house was so full of relatives and friends that the floor had to be reinforced under the living room. It caused some disturbance. I remember cousin Chet Schemper and I were waiting for the people to come. *The Grand Rapids Press* had arrived and so we looked at the newspaper headlines: the baby of Charles Lindbergh, the famous Trans-Atlantic flier, had been kidnapped on March 1.

I remember during the service in the house that our canary bird sang more than it should at a solemn time like that. The service was conducted by Rev. P. D. Van Vliet. It lasted about fifteen minutes and then the funeral procession went to the church. Pall bearers brought the casket to the hearse. What a lot of relatives and friends! When we reached the church, we found it to be filled to capacity. Pallbearers were his Sunday school class and honorary pallbearers were his school class from Holland Christian High School. I see some of those people once in a while yet today. The special music was by Betty Van Vliet who later married the Rev. Gary De Witt. I don't remember much of the service, but special mention was made about his diligence as a student by Dr. Garrett Heyns, the Superintendent of Holland Christian Schools at that time and an influential prison reformer.[50] Mention was also made of a poem that Arthur read at Young People's Society just two weeks before he died, called "God's Clock Keeps Time," and that was the epitaph on his grave stone: God's clock keeps time.[51]

54

God's Clock Keeps Time!

The signs are fast fulfilling for the coming of our Lord,
And sure are all the promises He's given in His word,
We know the time is near at hand when forces will combine
To persecute God's children, for "God's clock keeps time!"

The work goes on, but Oh, how prone we are to lethargy!
How sleepy and indifferent! How negligent to see
And understanding the meaning to our lives – both yours
and mine –
Of all the things that happen! – but "God's clock keeps time!"

We see the signs and wonders and we know they're pointing toward
The close of this world's history – to pestilence and sword;
To troubles with the nations; yet we settle down resigned
To take whatever cometh, though "God's clock keeps time!"

"God's clock keeps time!" What does that mean each day to
you and me?
Are we so fully ready to meet our Lord that we
Can settle down upon our ease and feel 'tis God's design,
And there is nothing we can do because His clock keeps time?

Arouse! Arouse, ye sleepers! Quick! Hasten to the work!
Go out and spread the message, stay not with those who shirk!
There are souls to gather everywhere, a harvest to refine,
Then let us gather quickly, for "God's clock keeps time!"

–Mina E. Carpenter

I believe it was providential that Art gave that message to the
young people at that time. It was such a nice thing to think back

on. I remember Art telling me to do certain things in life that he himself had done, pointing the way for me. It seemed he had some premonition about what was about to happen. God has His way of telling us, and sometimes we can't fully understand.

Arthur was going steady with a girl from the church. She took his death hard. I remember her walking to the cemetery at noon just to see his grave. But time healed; it wasn't long and she made some new acquaintance and married a classmate soon after she graduated.

I continued at Holland Christian, but it just wasn't the same. Brother Bill and Uncle Harry took the milk to the rusk factory every day. I stayed at my brother El and Henrietta's for a couple of weeks and then it was decided I was to take over the responsibility of delivering the milk. My turn had come. I had some experience with driving, but only very little.

It was decided that I could do the job by taking on some riders and have them help handle the creamery cans. Being only fifteen, I had to get a permit to drive. This meant a lot to my ego: I had to drive and take over a man's job. So that helped take away the lonesomeness I felt for Art. I missed him so much. He was my bed partner. I always looked up to him. I just couldn't appreciate high school after that.

Before I could take over the responsibility of delivering the milk, I had to get a permit to drive, and this meant to go to the chief of police and have him OK my driving. Believe it or not, it all went well. I got my permit on a Saturday. Uncle Harry and my dad were with me to make sure I got it. Holland's Chief of Police at that time was Pete Lievense, whose lap I sat on when he sold us the Nash about thirteen years earlier.

Well, on Monday I drove and all went well. I had to pick up someone at the library, which was upstairs at the Holland City Hall. The police station happened to be there also and, what do you know, a man yelled at me out of the large window and asked me to come in the station to show my license. I went in, and it

In Memoriam

ARTHUR NIENHUIS

*Whom the Lord called unto Himself on the 29th
day of February, in the year of Our Lord 1932.*

Arthur was a quiet, yet a good student. His school life was exemplary for youth, and his death, although a lesson for us, is a source of profound sorrow, both because he is no more with us and because of the loss to the bereaved.

Although likings and manifested in school life, love is not always seen on the surface, even if it is present. We did not state our love for Arthur when he was living, but it was nevertheless there.

We, therefore, wish to express ourselves in the sorrowful words of the poet which here apply so beautifully:

> *"For can we doubt, who knew thee keen*
> *In intellect, with force and skill*
> *To strive, to fashion, to fulfill —*
> *We doubt not what thou woulds't have been.*
>
> *We sometimes hold it half a sin*
> *To put in words the grief we feel;*
> *For words, like nature, half reveal*
> *And half conceal the soul within."*

—TENNYSON.

Arthur's memorial page from his Holland Christian High School yearbook

57

turned out the man calling to me was the same Pete Lievense that had given me the permit just two days earlier. Boy, I thought, what a poor memory! But he wanted to see that permit and I had to tell him I had left it in the rusk factory where I delivered the milk, and then came a reprimand. "Do not drive without it!" he said, and so it was another lesson learned.

Starting to drive was the beginning of a lot of new experiences. The minister's boys, Foster and Ted Van Vliet, rode with me for a small fee and they helped unload the creamery cans. I was small for my age. I had to sit on a pillow to drive and could barely reach the peddles, brake and clutch. There was no automatic transmission in them days. Of course, it was so good for my ego.

Just like that, I was grown up. Transportation to school in those days was mostly by car pool. There were very few vehicles there. I was available to help people: it was quite a convenience to have a "pick up" at school, and somebody who cared more about hauling stuff for school plays and taking teachers' wives here and there than studying.

Having a car also meant the beginning of dating. We had catechism on Wednesday nights and Young Peoples Society on Sunday nights. Although I wasn't very big, I was old enough and had many interesting experiences. Some I would like to share with you.

One of the first and most memorable dates I had was the result of a letter I received from a childhood sweetheart who I met going to grade school. She would come to her grandparents' house in Olive Township and visit our school and we really took advantage of those occasions, because I could only see her once in a while. Well, after I graduated from the grade school in Crisp, I didn't see her at all. Then a couple years passed, and I got a letter inviting me to come and see her in Grand Haven. She probably heard I could drive. I still have the letter.

She gave me the directions, but I wasn't going to make the trip alone, so I told cousin Chet Schemper about it. I was fifteen years old, but he was only thirteen and he said, "Let's go!" So plans were made and after Young Peoples Society on a Sunday night we went to Grand Haven. We had to go up some steps to a second-floor apartment and knocked on the door. I could hear her coming to the door and when it opened, I was looking at her waist. She had grown a foot since I saw her. So now what to do? She was pretty as ever, but where should we go? Well, she knew of a nice little park to go to, but Chet was with us. The vehicle was the 1928 Chevy that we made into a roadster for the evening, with an open back, so parking and sparking was kind of out of the question. After all, we hadn't seen each other for a couple of years, so we had a lot to talk about.

Well, Chet had already taken a few walks in the park and he was reminding me of the time a little bit by pointing to his watch, but for me time stood still. We finally decided to go back to the apartment and once again Chet went for a walk, but the problem was we just couldn't get talked out. This went on until she decided to go in. I asked what time it was; I seemed to have lost track. What a nice night we had, talking together.

So we finally went home. When we got home, it was 2:30 a.m., late for a couple of kids fifteen and thirteen, and we expected everybody to be up waiting for us. But to our surprise all was dark; everybody was sleeping. I dropped Chet off on the road and we made a little scheme: if they didn't hear him come home so late and he was able to sneak in, he said he would make the remark "Ho Hum Dinger" to me when I picked up the milk the next morning. Back at our house, I never went up the stairs so quiet as I did that night. The next morning, Chet came out with good strong "Ho Hum Dinger!" when he saw me.

So that was my first date, and after all it was quite a trip in those days, some twenty miles with an old '28 Chevy roadster. I had a few more dates with her after that, but my schedule wouldn't allow all that tripping. I didn't have enough money for gas. She had a girl-friend who would get some letters to me at Holland Christian High

59

School. She and her girlfriend would get together once in a while, and that way we would get word to one to another and keep in contact. Eventually, the letters stopped and I decided to go out with her friend who was the letter carrier, who I saw every day at Holland Christian. She was my first girl, but she was just a little older than me. She matured a lot faster than I did. She married while I was still in high school. I played the field for a number of years after that.

I always had an advantage in those tough years in the heart of the Depression, 1933 and '34.[52] Having a truck at school made it very convenient for a lot of kids to get a ride downtown with me. Many of these kids are now professors or doctors. I remember one church minister sharing some of those experiences while I served as an elder; he remembered how glad he was to have that ride downtown. Many of the riders were *Holland Sentinel* carriers in those days. The truck was loaded sometimes.

My brother El managed a Kroger store just four blocks from Holland Christian, which opened while I went to high school. I worked at the store for him after school. In those days, you waited on customers over a counter. The customer usually had a grocery list and you got what they asked for. Things had to be weighed and wrapped. There were long spools of string and you tied the packages. When you were through, you had to figure out what the bill was and you were paid in cash. Some of the customers were pretty hard to deal with. I don't think some of these people would put up with the bag boys of today.

During the time I went to Holland Christian, we had exceptionally good basketball players. We were state champions two of the four years I went to high school. This meant going to a lot of games. Five of the players on the team were in my class. Once again, transportation was the important thing, especially on dates. Quite often I went on double-dates after games with one of the ball players, because he was a minister's son and he was quite popular because of his stature and ability to play.

When I was in my second year in high school, my dad decided to buy a new Dodge pickup. The business at the rusk factory was picking up to the extent that they needed an additional amount of milk. I remember how excited I was to be driving a new 1933 Dodge pickup. It was the envy of a lot of people. That thing had the most wonderful purr to it, and it was the speediest car on the road. I would ride down that main road and open it up, and everybody could hear that car in the early morning. It really sounded nice, especially when it was loaded.

It wasn't long and I was competing with the truck in certain field trials, and that meant climbing steep hills. I was challenged to climb a hill north of town, and I made it and it was the talk of the school. I soon got to be known as the "Flying Challenger from Crisp."

We made many trips to Kalamazoo Field House, where the regional high school basketball games were played in them days. These were games everybody wanted to go to, so on one particular trip I had two with me inside the cab and three in the truck bed in back. We left the Tower Clock in Holland and one hour later we were inside the Kalamazoo city limits. We passed up everybody on the road and that was a mistake.

There was a very serious reprimand waiting for me the next day by the school superintendent, Dr. Heyns. He remarked about the speed I was driving when I passed them all on the road. I didn't believe I was as reckless as he said I was, but I did promise to be more careful from that time on. I believe the weather was the factor: it was raining and the faster I went, the drier the fellows in the back would stay, huddling against the back of the cab. Thinking back on it some, I'm thankful my guardian angel was looking over me. I have never had any serious accident, even as I write this.

We had many interesting times during those championship years. We had glory days. I remember going to Zeeland High School and making nuisances of ourselves, walking through the halls after they had been champions just one year earlier. There was a lot of rivalry with them in those days.

Another thing stands out in my memory during my high school years is a bank robbery that happened September 29, 1932 at First State Bank[53] in downtown Holland.

It just so happened that my Aunt Jennie Nienhuis[54] was one of many others who were in the bank when it happened. It was a very harrowing experience and caused quite a disturbance.

My friend, Chief of Police Pete Lievense, thought he would take a look to see what was happening. As he opened the door, he was shot in the stomach and that started a shoot-out that didn't stop without leaving one man seriously wounded and a number of others sent to the hospital. They were professional robbers from Chicago, including Lester Gillis, better known as "Baby Face Nelson."[55] It happened in the morning, so we headed downtown at noon to see what happened. Holland never had a robbery like it again. The police set up roadblocks, but the robbers took the side roads and got away with a lot of money and to this day I don't believe they ever were caught.

In January and February of 1936 was one of the worst blizzards this area has ever seen. I stayed in town in order to remain in school. If I had known that my life's partner was living right around the corner, I probably would have never got to Holland Christian High School.

It was the middle of March that I made arrangements to go home and see the mountains of snow. I went to the Holland Co-op which was on 7th or 8th Street at that time and got a ride with Harry Vander Zwaag, who lived in Crisp where the South Olive Church now stands.

It was a long trip home. We had to go to Hudsonville because all north-south roads were impassable, and I tell you, he had no intention of taking me all the way home. He parked his car by the old Nienhuis store and said, "We walk from here."

So I climbed up and down the huge drifts in the road. I walked along the telephone wires which were at least fifteen feet off the ground.

Bub and Dot at Reeds Lake in East Grand Rapids, site of Ramona Park
amusement park and several resorts, Decoration Day (Memorial Day), 1937

When I walked into the yard at home, there was a twenty-foot drift in front of the barn. But was it ever nice to be home sweet home. The family said that because the storms had let up, a bulldozer was going to try to clear the north and south main roads. So the next day, being Saturday, all of the available farmers in the neighborhood had to help shovel snow in front of the bulldozer plow. Uncle Bill, Clifford, Roger, my dad and brother Bill all were there to help.

I remember it was a real warm March day the next day, so we decided to walk to church, through the trail we made the day before. We got to church but we all had wet feet.

I graduated from Holland Christian in 1936 and had plans to go to Hope College, but the Depression made it impossible. Everybody was scratching for a living, let alone working my way through college. So I stayed home during what would have been my first year of college and worked on the farm.

I remember the night of graduation, driving our old 1927 Buick to Holland and having a difficult time finding a place to park. But whoever picked it up and drove it out of there didn't have that much trouble, because when we came out of the ceremony it was gone.

We reported it, and of course we couldn't tell them the license number, because we couldn't remember it, so the police had a difficult time locating it. The graduation party which the family had planned for me was kind of delayed. But I do remember they found the car in the ditch along one of the county roads south of Holland.

During my first year working full-time on the farm, President Roosevelt's programs were beginning to take effect. I remember when he declared a bank holiday to end a run on the banks in 1933,[56] and when he took the country off the gold standard the same year.

By the mid-1930s, we started to come out of the Great Depression. There were Works Progress Administration, or WPA, jobs for people who needed money to live. Welfare was not as available then as it was later. Many young men found opportunity to work in the Civilian Conservation Corps, or CCC, camps. These were reforestation projects set up by the government to replant the wastelands left over from when Michigan's big timber was cut decades earlier. Those lands were subject to a lot of erosion due to the chronic dry weather we experienced in those days. Just like there was the Dust Bowl in the West, we had dry weather in Michigan, too. I can remember cloudy days due to the dust storms out west. The CCC camps were run much like the army; fellows would sign up and be subject to all the regimentation necessary to keep things in order. They planted millions of trees which are full-grown trees today and are being used for lumber and pulpwood.

Roosevelt's programs were put into effect and proved to be as beneficial as they were meant to be. The bread lines began to disappear and, very slowly, things began to turn around economically and have improved ever since.

Many farmers found relief with the Federal Land Bank, which was set up specifically to provide credit for agriculture and keep farmers in business. This gave rural people more opportunity for borrowing, and in that, too, there was a big turn-around.

After I stayed home working on the farm for one year, I decided to go out and look for work together with cousin Chet, who had just finished the tenth grade. In our job hunt, we covered all the big towns, including Grand Rapids, Holland, Grand Haven, and Muskegon. We would go early in the morning and stand in line with fifty or more men, all wanting to work. Occasionally, personnel would come out and pick out a couple men that looked big and healthy and who had a friend or relative there for some pull. Chet and I got our first job in February 1937 at CWC – Campbell, Wyant & Cannon – a pit-fire foundry that made iron car parts such as engine blocks and camshafts. We were fortunate enough to have our cousin Harold Workman there pulling for us. He had just recently been hired in personnel after he graduated from high school. That was a godsend for us. Our applications were filled out and we were hired on the night shift.[57]

I started working on a Monday night. The Sunday night before that, I met the sweetest girl in all the world. Some fellows and I were taking our usual little ride around downtown Holland after Young Peoples Society. I had the privilege of going around with Julius Kamphuis, who always had a good car. That night there were four of us young men and three pretty girls decided to take a ride with us. They just happened to be walking the streets of Holland and we struck up a little conversation with them. One of them sat in the front between me and the driver, and we took some benefit curves on the corners as we drove around town.

One of the fellows riding with us suggested we pick up his car at the church. At this time, Julius Kamphuis decided to go home as he was without a girl.

After he left, that girl and I spent the rest of the night getting acquainted in the back seat of a car which I didn't own while the other occupants visited the nearby Log Cabin Tavern. That's how I met my new girlfriend, Dorothy or "Dot" Van Langevelde, and that's how these sixty-two years together began.

We decided to make a date for the following Thursday night, but the next morning is when Chet and I got our jobs at CWC and we had to work nights, so I had to break our first date. That was a very difficult thing for me to do, as I really wanted to see Dot, but the importance of my job for the family outweighed this. The next Saturday night, we made up for it.

At CWC, I was hired in the wire room. The wires I made had to be bent to fit sand cores that were made to be put in molds that formed Ford motor blocks for the new 1937 V8 cars.

Chet Schemper and I started together and it all was a new experience. In those days, the work day was as long as the company wanted to make it. Most of the time we worked twelve-hour nights from 3:30 p.m. to 3:30 in the morning.

I was needed on the farm, but since I was giving my checks to the family I was allowed to go out and work. The farm and all its operations were desperately in need of financial assistance. I remember how proud I was with my first paycheck: it was forty dollars for the first two weeks I put in.[58] I laid the check on the table when I got home, and when they got up in the morning my dear parents were just thrilled. They couldn't believe that I could make so much money for two weeks' work.

Chet and I worked for about a year before we were laid off. The first thing I remember my dad buying was a team of horses at a farm sale: strawberry roans, Maud and May. What a beautiful team. With a little money, things were different on the farm. It was decided to buy a new car. The old 1927 Buick had had it and the new cars were so much improved. The decision was left up to me as I was the one paying for it.

We went to all the dealers in Holland, to the Ford and Chevy and Dodge, and finally wound up at the Hudson dealer. This was the car for me: the Hudson Terraplane. It had an Electric Hand on the steering post to shift it. This was something out of this world. It had the long-stroke piston, eight-cylinder engine. It was the nicest riding and speediest car on the road.

Well, with that new car and having a good paying job, my courtship with Dorothy got to be all the more real. We had an occasional argument, but true love never runs smooth. Still, our being together got to be all the more frequent.

Around this time, my cousin Chet and I also decided to take music lessons. We went out and bought new guitars: I got a Dobro and he bought a Gibson, so I played Hawaiian style and he played Spanish. We had a lot of fun doing this. We played in an orchestra led by our music instructor, Dean Mokma. We sang and played in Young Peoples Society and school P.T.A.s.[59]

Our year at the foundry was a very prosperous year for the both of us, and then a recession set in and we were laid off. So once again we were on meager fare. Of course, there was always the farm to fall back on, which was a lot of work but not much pay.

It was in the year 1938 that Uncle Harry – Chet's dad – Chet, and myself decided to go into business. All the time that I wasn't with Dorothy, my wife-to-be, I spent with Chet. We were always together. We saw molds advertised as a way to go into the novelty business, and we knew a little about making objects from molds as part of our foundry work. We read up on various procedures and then we sent for molds out of which we could make some artifacts such as crucifixes, busts of certain prominent people, and various Dutch gadgets that might be popular for Holland's Tulip Time celebration.

We started with lead crucifixes. We invested in molds. We had a forge in which we could melt lead. This melted lead was poured into these molds and left to cool. After it hardened, we would remove them from the mold and paint them. That was my part of the job. I was appointed chief painter and decorator. I got pretty good at that even if I do say so myself.

Chet was in charge of sales. He corresponded with a lot of large companies and stores and it wasn't long before we started to get orders. I remember our first order from Woolworth's, a five-and-ten-cent store: the order was for a thousand crucifixes. Making them was no problem, but shipping them was something else. We should have packed them separately in boxes and then packed the boxes in a large box. Instead, we put them all of them together in one large box and not enough thought was put into the handling of a thousand lead crucifixes. The box weighed about three hundred pounds. When we dropped it off at the freight depot in Holland, we began to have second thoughts as to how the railroad people would handle that weight. We found out a couple weeks later: we put a lot of warnings on our box, such as "Handle With Care," and "Do Not Tip," but they were not heeded. Apparently, our shipment arrived in a damaged state.

The profit margin on something like that was so small that we couldn't afford to continue on in the business world with that venture, so we decided to look into the new discovery of plastics. We started ordering plastic molds for book ends and busts of Dutch boys and girls for Tulip Time in Holland.

In order to sell, we had to name our business; we decided to call it the Holland Ornamental and Novelty Works. Chet was the sales manager. We had two separate buildings to work out of and we spent the first six months of 1937[60] making all kinds of stuff. We had a lot of book ends and Dutch boy and girl stuff out on consignment. All went well until we needed some additional investment. We advertised and had very little response, as we were just coming out of the Depression. So when field work began again in the spring, we decided to close down for a while.

It was at this time that a couple gentlemen arrived from Chicago and expressed some interest in our business, but it so happened that Chet the sales manager was in the creek, barefoot, watering the horses at the time they arrived. I guess it left a bad impression or something, as our business never did get started again after that. Money was just too hard to get. Our business went defunct; the hard times were still with us. We had spent about a year working on Holland Ornamental & Novelty, and when it went belly-up I wound up owing about $250 to our business partner, Chet's dad, my Uncle Harry.

I spent the summer on the farm after that. Brother Bill and I had five acres of pickles that we would pick ourselves, just for something to do. I made about sixty dollars and Bill a little less, if I remember correctly. I do remember something very important that happened at that time: thanks to FDR – President Roosevelt – an unemployment compensation law was passed. Since Chet and I had been laid off at Campbell, Wyant & Cannon, we were entitled to sixteen dollars for sixteen weeks. Whoa! We went to the newly organized Employment Service, and found out we were entitled to the maximum benefit because of our good wages earned.

We were interviewed and required to be looking for work to collect. I remember getting my first check. My brother Bill shook hands with me; he couldn't believe it, getting money for not doing anything. In those days, you were lucky to have a job that paid sixteen dollars a week, let alone getting paid that amount while doing absolutely nothing for it. That was the beginning of the Democratic handout. I sure was glad I voted for Franklin Roosevelt.

Chet and I fared pretty well the rest of the summer, working on the farm and helping out our folks, who were trying so hard to make ends meet.

In the fall, after the Heinz pickle factory closed, we would hand-pack pickles for shipping to other buyers. We took them to Holland Motor, who hauled them to the Chicago market, and we couldn't wait for the mail man to deliver the results over the following days. There was a lot of demand for those pickles. People wanted them for canning, which was very popular in those days, especially in the big city where people couldn't grow food themselves.

Yes, even as I went through successes and failures, Dorothy and I continued our courtship and we started to make plans to get married. On a beautiful June day, my wife's parents, Herman and Hattie Van Langevelde, decided to make the trip out to the country and see where I hailed from. I remember that afternoon as if it were yesterday. We all gathered around our kitchen table on 124th Avenue to have fresh homemade bread with strawberries. Although Dorothy's mother was having a lot of health problems at that time, she was exceptionally well that afternoon.

Dot and I were spending more and more time together. Rather than make all those trips back and forth to her family home in Holland, she decided to stay at our house most of the time. There was always so much more going on at our place, although I would stay in Holland, too, occasionally, if we had reason to save a trip that way. Dot was also part of a large family: her parents had Peter, Bernard, Clarence, Frances, Alice, Gertrude, Dorothy and Bette.[61]

I remember so well that same night, after Dot's parents came out to the farm to visit, we were awakened in the middle of the night by Uncle John Altena and Gabriel Kuite,[62] uncle and

Elegant wedding photo, December 9, 1938

brother-in-law of the wife. We had get over to Dot's family home in Holland immediately, as my dear fiancée's mother had a severe stroke and wasn't expected to live.

The family had to be called together as her conditioned worsened. It was left to me to go get Dot's brother Bernard from Cassopolis, where he was living in railroad quarters as he was employed by the Pere Marquette Railway at the time. My wife's brother Clare[63] and I went after him.

We had just bought the Hudson Terraplane brand new and this was the time to find out what it had. We went as fast as we could, because we wanted Bern to see his mother alive if at all possible. That Hudson Terraplane went 90 MPH most of the way up and back. We did get him home in time to see her pass away. She never uttered another word after ten o'clock the night before.

The family had already experienced some very hard times. It was only three months earlier, in March, that the family had a very sad experience. Dot's oldest brother, Pete, had been experiencing a lot of problems. He had suffered a kidney infection when he was younger and it never healed, but instead developed into a serious kidney condition called Bright's Disease.

This particular incident occurred on March 12, 1938.[64] Earlier that same day, Dot and I and a couple other girls went to a basketball tournament game in Kalamazoo. It was tournament time and Holland Christian was playing St. Augustine at the Kalamazoo Fieldhouse. Holland Christian won the game. We returned home around ten o'clock to find Dot's family waiting for us to tell us the bad news: Brother Pete had passed away at Zeeland Hospital. He walked into the hospital feeling ill and died shortly after he entered. What a shock for the family, especially his parents Herman and Hattie, not realizing his condition was that serious. He was 27 and married to a woman named Rose, and worked in a coal yard in town.[65]

It was a year of sorrow for Dot's dad: He lost his oldest son in March, and his wife in June, and his father-in-law in the fall, all in the same year, 1938.

Still, despite these losses, life went on. Dot's sister Gertrude, whose nickname was "Honey," and became known mostly as "Hon,"[66] went ahead with her plans to be married in November. So Dot and I decided to marry on December 9 of that same year.[67]

It was at this time that Dot's dad decided to move out of the old house on Ninth Street in Holland. It was an old house, a brown shack by the railroad tracks in town, and they needed a change. They moved to a much better home and took with them all the memories that big family enjoyed. Clare went into the Civilian Conservation Corps and then was drafted into the army during World War II. Bern was away from home most of the time, working for the railroad.

A new chapter in my life was about to begin. Dot and I decided to say our vows in my parents' house on 124th Avenue, the home where I had lived all my younger days. The Rev. P. D. Van Vliet, then minister of South Olive Christian Reformed Church, conducted the ceremony. Most everybody married at home in those days, because of the poor state of affairs. It was still Depression and you did only what you could afford. We beautified the home with all kinds of greenery and bark taken from the Pigeon Creek area. A friend of my wife's, Bill Bennet,[68] made an arch that we decorated with pine branches and flowers. My brother Clifford was my best man, and my wife's younger sister Bette was her bride's maid. I remember waiting for the signal to come downstairs and march through the kitchen and through the sitting room into the parlor. Of course, Dot did likewise, to the song "Here Comes the Bride" sung by a girlfriend of Bette's, Marion Mouw. They also sang a couple popular wedding songs, "Oh Promise Me," and "I Love You Truly."[69]

We had a house full of relatives and friends. While we were having the reception, suddenly there was a lot of noise going on outside! The shivareeners[70] had arrived and they didn't quiet down until I went out there to pay them off. All the fellows that I had gone with to so many weddings were gathered there, and then a few more. It was quite a bill to pay, but it was worth it. People played tricks on the wedding couple in them days, and sometimes right back on the shivareeners, too: I remember one place, we were standing next to a house and got drenched by a couple pails of water thrown from an upstairs window.

Well, it was a nice home wedding and our honeymoon had to be postponed, as the tires on the car were too poor to travel anywhere. All the money we had went into our wedding, so that had to be put off until later.

After our wedding, we went to bed right at home. How well we remember! We got to our bridal bed and it reeked of onions. Dot's older sister knew neither one of us liked onions and had filled the bed with them. So, we had to change the sheets before we finally could get to sleep.

The next morning, we got an invite to go on a tour with my folks through the Holland St. Louis Sugar Company factory, where we brought our sugar beets for many years. It was a very interesting experience, and also the sweetest thing on earth we could do. So that was one honeymoon trip that we took together.

On Monday of the next week, Chet and I started to look for work. Campbell, Wyant & Cannon wasn't calling us back, and now that I was married I needed a job.

We watched the Grand Rapids area for employment ads. There was one ad from Bennett Pump Co. looking for a machine sand molder to work in Grand Rapids. This was somewhat related to what we'd done at CWC, so we applied and got the job. I had experience making cores at CWC, so I had a core-making job, while Chet was put on the sand molding machine. We worked a couple days when Chet was put to the real test: his supposed know-how didn't work.[71] There was a big explosion of sand and a noise that shook the plant, and Chet was fired. I decided I'd walk out with him and that was the end of that.

We continued to look for work and Chet landed a job at Challenge Machinery in Grand Haven, where they made tools for the printing industry such as paper cutters and drills, and quite soon after that, I got a job at the Bastian-Blessing Company in Grand Haven. My job consisted of buffing and polishing stainless steel soda fountains for ice-cream parlors. These products were beautiful and were sent all over the world. My starting wage was forty cents an hour and I believed it to be an answer to prayer. Being married and all, I had to have a job.

We were married a few months when morning sickness set in for my dear wife and, of course, she was in the family way. Because of the Depression and a slow recovery, our first years of marriage were spent living with my folks on the farm on 124th Avenue. There was plenty of work on the farm. It didn't pay too much, but at least we had a roof over our heads and plenty to eat.

We were expecting our first child in February of 1940. According to Dr. VandenBerg's regular check-ups on my wife, everything seemed perfectly normal. She carried the baby the full nine months, but then her pregnancy went on longer than it should have. We waited a couple of weeks and then a scary thing happened: her water broke at home and we rushed her to the hospital.

Things happened fast. I remember the doctor looking up at me and saying, "Things are not looking right; probably you would sooner leave." I was shocked, but determined to stay with Dot and see it through. Our baby girl was still-born on February 13. It was terrible hard for us. There were all kinds of happy expectations dashed to pieces, but our pastor and so many came to console us.

My dad and I went to the funeral home and arranged for the burial of our first darling little baby. We were convinced of God's way being the best way. That was when my dad shared with me for the first time the story of my own birth, when he and mother had been afraid they might lose me. And yet, here I was, and there was hope that good things would happen for us, too.

We weathered that storm together, and things began to change not too long after that.

We lived with the folks for about three years when we heard that Uncle Bill and Aunt Martha Kooyers were thinking about moving out of our family's other farm home on Tyler Street and buying a farm of their own. Uncle Bill had been working at the Limbert Company[72] quite steady and saved enough to buy a farm. They thought it would be a nice place for Dot and I to live and that we did.

It was such a big change, and how strange it seemed to be on our own. It was a wonderful experience. I remember those first days: we had a pitcher pump in the kitchen and we pumped our water. We had a coal and wood stove to cook and bake and keep warm with. We had an oil-burning space heater in the living room. It was real nice and cozy living there for our first years together. Of course, we had to have a dog and his place was under the house on the west side. There was a crawl space under half of the old house on the east side, which was our cooling area. It was an old Michigan cellar, as they called it in them days. We would put stuff on the floor down there to keep it fresh. We had no refrigerator in those days.

My parents agreed that we could do chores for the rent, so I always had cows to milk and horses to feed. Very soon, I started working full-time at Bastian-Blessing, so that meant early rising. I would get up at four o'clock to milk the cows by hand and feed them, and then do the same thing at night, and it all worked real well for a number of years. We had a car pool to get back and forth to work in Grand Haven. Each person would take their turn driving. I did have a conflict at times, because Dot and I needed to share our only car with my brother Clifford, who worked also. So sometimes I walked a couple miles to get a ride to work.

Cousin Chet and I still had a lot to do with each other. We rode to work together, though he worked at Challenge Machinery. While he was working there, Chet decided to finish high school and go on to college. He did this by going to night school for a year and then quit his job and went to Calvin College.

Bub and Dot, with Bub proudly showing off his heart-shaped ring

War clouds were gathering in Europe, which was being overrun by the Nazis. Hitler had taken over Austria in 1938, and then Czechoslovakia and Poland in 1939, and then the old country of Holland in 1940. One country of after another was being taken over and plundered.

Our country was becoming more involved. Young men were being drafted. All American men between the ages of eighteen and forty had to register. Men with no dependents were eligible for the draft, and every man got one of dozens of different classifications, from 1-A – meaning they were eligible to serve – to 4-F, which meant they were found to be unable to serve for health reasons. Every available young man that was healthy enough was called into service, and joined either the Army, Navy or Marines. Many signed up for the Merchant Marine, which is a peacetime shipping operation that switches to delivering troops and war supplies by boat during wartime.

It was at this time that our first son, Marlan, was born. This was something we really looked forward to because of the disappointment we had endured with our first child. Dot had a tough, hot summer to live through in 1941 and it was in the fall that we finally reached the time to go to the maternity home of Mrs. Lampen.[73] We had made arrangements ahead of time to go to her place when the time came, and I remember sitting down by our old pump organ and playing "What a Friend We Have in Jesus" while my dear wife was packing her bags and getting ready for the new arrival. It was that next morning at ten minutes to 11 a.m., on October 11, that Marlan was born. What a miracle! What a wonderful answer to our prayers! A good, healthy baby boy.

Mrs. Lampen was the mid-wife at this maternity home. In those days, people avoided the hospital because of the cost. She was a registered nurse and was licensed to do this. I was at the bedside through the whole procedure. I believe the cost was no more than twenty-five dollars and the mother stayed in bed for ten days. If the baby could be nursed, it was done as long as possible.

I believe Dot nursed Marlan for at least a year. It sure was swell to come home from work to our own little family.

Of course, our darling little baby had to be baptized and that was usually done quite soon after birth, because then it would be less disturbance, less crying at the service. It was on a Sunday, December 7, that we chose to have this done. It was at the after-noon service, which started at two o'clock. Our pastor at the time was the Rev. P. D. Van Vliet. There were three couples there baptizing new babies: Lester Dams,[74] Lawrence Prince, and our-selves. The whole procedure went well for us, but the others got to be pretty noisy. But we got this all taken care of. Of course, our closest friends were there to enjoy it with us.

Those friends and relatives came over to our house afterward for coffee and we spent that evening with Dot's sister and brother-in-law, Hank and Hon, with their little girl Marla and the folks. It was a big day for more than just one reason: a special bulletin came over the radio while we were listening to a program and said Pearl Harbor was being attacked by the Japanese. That was the begin-ning of the worst war this world has ever seen.

I remember riding to work the next day with a whole car full of eligible fellows that sooner or later would all be called to the army. It was uppermost on all our minds as we drove that sooner or later our freedom would be gone.

The next day, our President Franklin Delano Roosevelt, the greatest president this country has ever seen, announced on the radio that war was declared on Japan. Our entire fleet stationed at Pearl Harbor was destroyed, along with about 3000 precious lives.

Knowing what you would do in the war was just a matter of waiting for your classification. Everybody under forty years old was notified. Draft boards were set up in each county all across the country. Those who were married and had dependents would be classified 1-B or 1-C. Farming was considered war essential, as were the defense jobs in local factories.

As the war continued, we also declared war on Germany and so thousands were called. The newspapers had many listed as dead or missing. Gold stars were being hung in the windows, which designated that someone in that household was killed or missing. Almost every day, there was someone in the news that had been killed or was missing. Four of our cousins were killed in action. They were all fellows my age or younger. Gerard Looman was a pilot and was killed while flying over the Romanian oil fields. They found his remains there years later and I remember going to that funeral. My Aunt Johanna (Kooyers) and Uncle Manley Looman felt so bad. He was their only son. Leon Nienhuis, a cousin who worked with me at CWC, was drafted early and lost his life at the Battle of the Bulge. Rick Reinder, a cousin from Chicago, was killed in the Italian campaign. Another cousin, Bud Van Til,[75] lost his life in the Pacific Theater.

As the war continued, brother Clifford was drafted. He had been married about a year when he got his greetings. He passed his physical in Detroit, where everyone went to find out if they were accepted for duty. Those who weren't physically fit would be sent home as 4-Fs.

It was a sad day when my parents and a bunch of us took Cliff to Grand Haven, where he joined a bus load of draftees. All the men lined up and were given Bibles and they were on their way after prayers and God's blessing was said by the representative from the Gideons. Then all the well-wishing and hugs and kisses were done and we watched the bus leave and we waved our sad goodbye.

I drove on the way home, and very little was said. Mother and Dad really felt the impact of the occasion, and when mother got home and saw that half cup of coffee that brother hadn't finished, it really brought out the tears. Dear Mother felt so bad. It all looked so hopeless at that time, as we were losing the war.

There were many at that time that were called draft dodgers, who tried to get out of their service. Some of the men I knew were able to get farm deferments, as we needed the food for the war

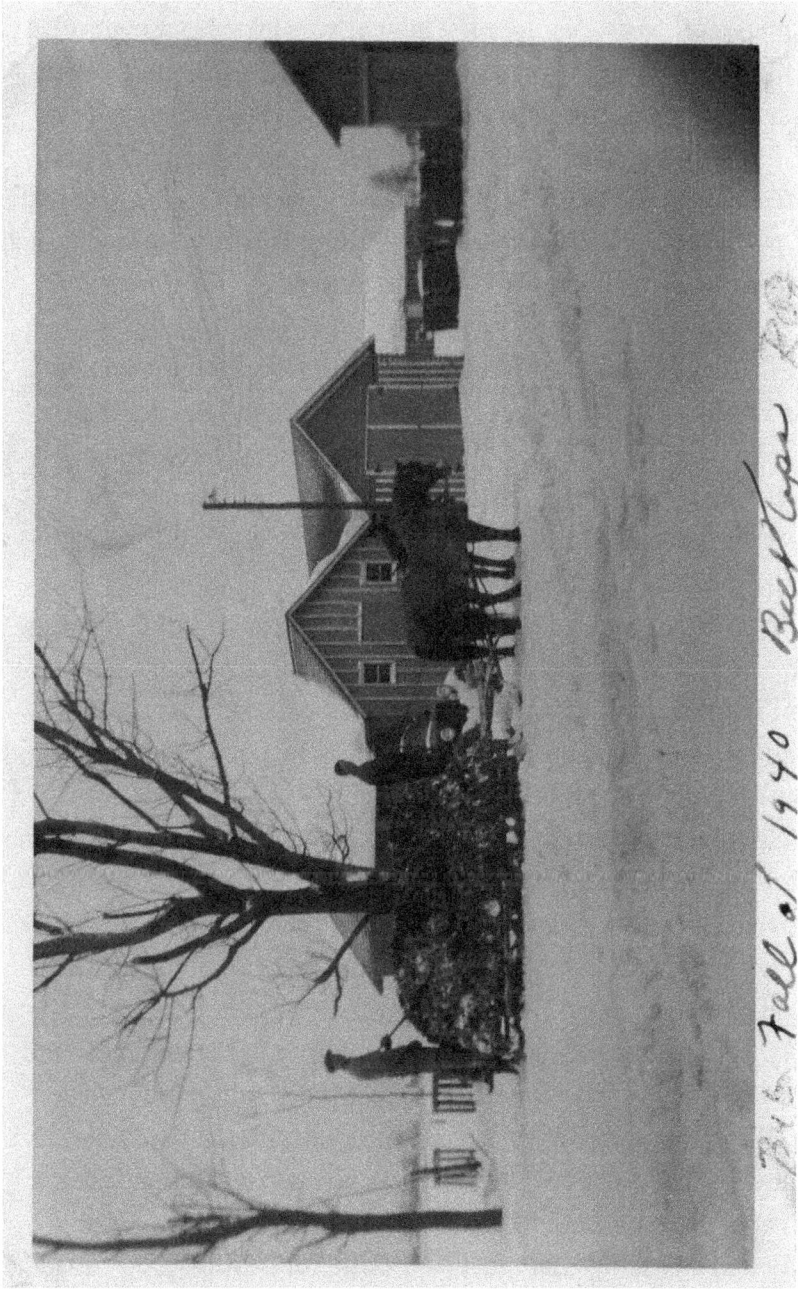

Bub (left) and Fog with a sleigh piled with beet tops on the homestead, 1940

effort. Some jobs were war essential, with many factories converted to defense work. Before the war was over, we all took the trip to Detroit to be examined. The war was just about over when I got my greetings. I, of course, was older than Cliff and Roger and I had three dependents, children Marlan and Nancy and the wife. I was working in a defense plant along with the farming, to my credit, which was given quite a bit of consideration. I also had some physical disqualifications which I found out after my physical in Detroit. The war ended quite soon after this.

My brother Clifford was in the service about a half-year when my dad suffered a fatal heart attack. My brother Rog and I were doing the farming on the big family farm while my dad remained overseer. Rog had a farm deferment from the draft and I was also requested by the draft board to live up to my requirement to remain on the farm.

My brother Rog and I were hauling manure for pickles on June 10, 1943,[76] when my dad decided to put up a temporary fence for our milk cows; we had some forty head of cattle at that time, and he wanted to open up more grazing, as it was a very wet spring and the land could not be worked.

While he was putting up the fence, he disappeared. After some waiting, we finally figured one of us should look for him and me, being the oldest, went along the road and then along the fence row. I found him with his little dog licking his face. I grabbed his shoulder and his head flopped. I knew he was dead.

My mother and brother Rog were waiting in the distance, and I yelled to them it was all over. We called the family and the coroner. Gilbert VandeWater was the county coroner at that time, and he came with brother El. Doctor Nykamp also was called, and he confirmed the fact that he died of a heart attack.

My dad's passing changed everything for brother Rog and me. The family was now our responsibility. It wasn't just the farm work, which we were already doing; my dad had always been involved in church work. He had taught Sunday school for some thirty years and had been part of the church consistory, and so it was necessary to replace him. When he died, his work had all been taken care of for the coming week, but there was only a week and then there had to be someone new to take over. The church appointed Ben Brandsen to take his place, but it was not too long after that that he also died of a heart attack.

During the time that we were pastored by Rev. Titus Heyboer,[77] I was confronted by one of the faithful elders, Henry Zwiers, and asked if I would consider taking over the responsibility of being superintendent of the Sunday school. I accepted that job, and with the encouragement of Rev. Heyboer, I served as superintendent for ten years.

Those were very rewarding years; the teaching and the meetings with the other teachers were occasions for real spiritual growth. Most of those teachers have now passed on to glory. Their testimonials have left an impact on our children who now are celebrating the effects in the lives of their own children. I started that work while Rev. Heyboer was pastor and I stopped during the time of Doctor Theodore Minnema.[78] Sunday School was always very well attended, with one hundred to 150 students every week.

After Dad's passing, responsibility for the farm was left to me and to my brother Rog, who was seven years younger than me. Mother's health was good and we relied on her a lot. The war was still at its worst and it was a time when farm help was hard to come by, and Rog and I believed we should be able to appeal to the military to get brother Clifford back out of service and have him help us on the farm. We succeeded in doing this, and so we managed quite well that summer.

The first thing we had to do in order to make our new family situation work was to remodel: my mother and father's place, which we always referred to as "the homestead," was made into a two-family dwelling. Cliff and his wife Geneva had the upstairs, and mother and Rog lived downstairs. Dot and I had the other farmhouse down the road on Tyler.

They lived that way for a couple years and then Clifford decided to buy a neighboring farm, an eighty-acre outfit with some build- ings called the Lester Dams Place. Cliff had his farm deferment and so he lived up to his military obligation there and we continued as we had before. But we had some poor farming weather for a year or two and it seemed we had difficulty making ends meet. All of us were more or less bound to the farming by the war effort.

Because the farming was bad, we performed our duty by joining the war workforce again at Campbell, Wyant & Cannon.[79] Everything they did there was defense work. Taking these jobs was a way to keep our expenses paid and keep the farms going. Everything you did had to be reported to the draft board and then re-classification would follow.

Clifford had a very rough time on his eighty-acre farm, which he bought for $8000. A year or two of poor returns on the farm work made him decide to apply for work at CWC, which had to be okayed by the draft board because of his honorable discharge a couple years earlier. Later on, he did quit farming, but he stayed at CWC for thirty years and retired with a nice pension.

Brother Rog and I decided to farm as Nienhuis Brothers and to buy the homestead from Mother together. But our decision to buy it out was a bigger problem than we expected: our dad did not have the farm on a joint deed with Mother, so it took a long time with a lot of red tape to get that done. My mother couldn't do anything without all Father's brothers' and sisters' say-so. So this procedure got to be a whole lot longer than we cared for, with many meet- ings with lawyers and family before it was decided how much it all would cost. We did finally buy the farm and buildings and tools for $14,000. It was a very reasonable deal. We bought twenty acres along with it, so we had about 210 acres. Our older brother El helped get a lot of that done, and thanks to him we farmed quite successfully for seven years as Nienhuis Brothers.

84

I was told by the township treasurer that we were the largest landowners in the township at that time. How true that was is questionable. Farming as Nienhuis Brothers, we had over one hundred head of cattle, about one hundred hogs, and a couple thousand chickens. Rog was in charge of field work and I was in charge of all the manual chores, such as caring for the livestock and hauling milk. We had a good market for our milk. The Holland Rusk Company, which later was bought out by National Biscuit Co., took all our milk along with that of a number of other farmers in the neighborhood. We sold milk to the rusk plant for some twenty-five years. We supplied them with twelve 10-gallon cans a day. A very good way to sell milk. I had a regular milk route five days a week during that time, and I remember all the passengers that took advantage of that trip to Holland. Quite often they would be standing on the road waiting for a lift to Holland.

Our oldest son Marlan Lee was really caught up in this Nienhuis Brothers enterprise. He was a year-and-a-half old when my dad died, and so he more or less grew up working the farm with his Uncle Rog, who had him driving the tractor when he was five years old.

We hayed at that time with a hay loader and that meant two men loaded and one on the tractor drove very slowly. Marlan was five at the time and he wanted to drive the tractor, a Farmall H, which we let him do. It was remarkable how well he did for a child his age. I remember him driving and the tractor choked going through a ditch. Standing up while he drove, he managed to start the tractor and keep going. Unbelievable what that little guy could do and how much he helped us. When there was tractor work, he was there. I remember helping Rog plow a twenty-acre piece that was square. Marlan was very discouraged about the fact that he couldn't make the corner right, compared to his Uncle Rog who was ahead of him plowing with our Ford Ferguson. I told him, "Just make fun of it and forget it; what you can't do the disk will do."

Marlan in front of the Tyler Street farm

I managed all our chores at that time and all the other business connected to farming, and Marlan and Rog kept the machinery going. Marlan was our helper until his Uncle Rog lost his life in the accident that happened later.

The war was winding down in 1945[80] and it was pretty evident that we, the Allies, were going to be victorious. Things were changing for the better fast, as our military forces had the situation well in hand. It was at the end of the war that many of the older available men were drafted. A brother-in-law, Ray Van Vorst, was called and he joined the Marines and put in two years. Brother-in-law Clare Van Langevelde came home with an honorable discharge after four years of service. It was a wonderful time to see the men come home. Many welcome parties were held.

It was in the month of April that same year that our great President Roosevelt died of a cerebral hemorrhage. It shocked the nation and put many people in mourning. He was one of the greatest presidents this country had ever seen. The terrible Depression was over and people had plenty of work and the war had even created a shortage of help.

It was soon time for our Vice President Harry S. Truman to take over. I listened to his acceptance speech on the radio, taking the oath of office, and heard him in his humble way speak of his incapabilities – but he soon got a grip on it all. It was him who had to decide about the use of the atom bomb and when and where. He soon made up his mind to destroy the main Japanese munitions cities of Nagasaki and Hiroshima. We evened the score and then some as our loss at Pearl Harbor was avenged. The war in the Pacific ended quite soon after that.

Our brother-in-law Ray Van Vorst went back to volunteering on the fire department when he came home, and while being at a fire he suffered a severe heart attack. Shortly after that, he had another heart attack at the barber shop on a Saturday morning, and he was rushed to Holland Hospital and died. This was a terrible shock to all of us. He was only 28 years old and had just come out of the Marines. His dear wife had an awful hard time dealing with that; after all those years in service, they were just happily back together and then he died. His funeral was at the Sixth Reformed Church in Holland. I remember the song sung at his funeral, "Beyond the Sunset." Rev. Mouw[81] preached the sermon.

It was after the war that farming was good and Rog and I, as Nienhuis Bros., were farming in a pretty good profitable way. Roger and his wife, Gladys, were married in June of 1946, and decided to live at the homestead where he had lived with my mother ever since Dad died.

Our family went from Marlan to Nancy to Robert to Jack in those days on the farm. Nancy was born during the war, and Bob was born December 10, 1945, and that happened at the same time that the North Holland Church burned, quite soon after the end of the war. My brother Rog and I were working at Campbell, Wyant & Cannon foundry in the winter time. Sort of burning the candle at both ends, as the saying goes. Our son Jack was born the following year on Feb. 3. We moved the following year to make room for our growing family.

Clifford and Geneva's apartment at the homestead had been rented by a newly married couple, but soon that couple moved on. It was at this time that Dot and I decided to move up there in that apartment with our family, so that we could build a new home on our place on Tyler. Our family had been growing and we thought the old house we lived in had to be replaced. So we decided to move upstairs at the homestead while we made plans for that, but once again things got to be a little too tough.

After we lived there for some time, our daughter Karen was born. It was rather crowded upstairs at the homestead, with the seven of us, but it was also nice as brother Rog and Gladys also had a young growing family. So our kids and their kids had a lot in common growing up together. We had some wonderful years on the farm.

Nienhuis kids on the homestead with the pickup they called the "ol' truckee." (foreground, left to right) Nancy, cousin Dave Nienhuis, Marlan; (in truck bed) Bob, Jack. Barely visible is Bub behind the wheel of the pickup.

We rented our farmhouse for a year or so and then decided to move back, as we didn't have the money to build a new house and things didn't look too promising. The upstairs apartment at the homestead was a little too small for all seven of us.

My Uncle Will and Aunt Hattie Nienhuis lived to the south of us, and they were getting older. They meant a lot to me, as we grew up with them. My parents and them were very close and did many things together and he and my dad had a lot in common as brothers. My dad had four brothers and they all lived in the immediate vicinity, so threshing and all manual tasks were shared.

Uncle Will's first wife died when she was in her early forties. What a shock: it left him with one boy, who was the oldest, and three girls, the youngest of whom was seven. At that time, Uncle Will was working at the Holland Furnace Company, which was the leading maker of coal home furnaces in the country, so he was gone during the day. That meant the oldest boy had to do the farming. It was a very difficult time, as Uncle Will had to deal with the day-to-day struggles along with the memories. My mother helped all she could and kept them very close to us through those years.

At this time, many things were done by horse and sleigh in the winter time. I remember my dad and Uncle Will butchering and going all the way to Grand Haven with their product for some ready cash in those tough Depression days.

By the time Dot and I and our young family were living upstairs at the homestead, Uncle Will couldn't farm anymore because of his advanced age. So Rog and I decided to rent his farm, which bordered ours.

Uncle Will, being in his seventies, was developing some dementia or hardening of the arteries, as it was called in those days. He just loved to get into his old 1927 Dodge and ride over to our house, but his ability to drive was becoming very seriously curtailed by his poor judgment and he wound up in the daydream ditch once too often and so from that time on he came over on foot.

Jack, Bob, Nancy and Roger's son Dave enjoy an O-So pop out in a freshly mowed hayfield. Notes on photo say "1950 Oct 21, 2nd cut."

Aunt Hattie, his second wife, was quite a bit younger and she had her hands full with him. She would usually call whenever he left for our place so that we would watch for him and yell for him to stop in, as otherwise he would get lost. Uncle Will was always humorous about his mistakes and was quite easy to handle and was a lot of company to us. He would always want to help us in whatever we were doing but his thinking became more and more impaired.

It was at this time that we decided as a church community in Olive Township to begin a Christian elementary school.[82] Most of the children in Olive went to public schools and then transferred to Holland Christian High School if they could afford it. But consolidation was taking place in the public school system, and the handwriting was on the wall: the youth would have to be bussed to larger schools. Christian influence in the schools would be seriously curtailed, and instruction would be atheistic in content. It was time for church people to put their foot down. Separation of church and state would be emphasized.

Many meetings were held. I was among many church members across the township who helped organize our own Christian School Society. Our pastor at South Olive CRC, the Rev. Seibert Kramer, was instrumental in organizing this society in our area, and Reformed Church members as well as Christian Reformed were invited.

In the middle of this work, the Rev. Kramer received a call to go to another church, but quite soon our vacancy was filled by the Rev. Titus Heyboer. As soon as he got used to us as a congregation, he continued what Rev. Kramer had started. A local school board was formed and things started to happen.

This was the beginning of the years when I burned the midnight oil. It just so happened that I was on the first Christian School Board for our area, and it was not easy. I served with Jake Brandsen, Gilbert Hop and John Bowman. We decided to have collections in church and canvas the area for support. This work was not all that promising at first, but the dedication and prayers of a few made the progress of our new Christian school a reality in our community.

After a year of planning and meeting, the Rev. Heyboer and board decided to begin our very own Christian school in the chapel of our church. It was voted on and accepted by the congregation and so our Christian school began that next fall, in 1951.

At that time there were many opposed, including many in the church consistory, but it did finally work out in the end. Right prevailed over wrong.

Consolidation of school districts began taking place and children started going further away to schools, and this put even more emphasis on our work. Many wondered if they were doing the right thing, as it was a tremendous cost to put the kids in our own school. But all managed to work it one way or another, and some never paid all of their tuition, but it did become a wonderful reality. My heart goes out to Rev. Heyboer, who did so very much to make our South Olive Christian school a reality. His foresight and determination made our school what it is today.

It was decided to have school in the church chapel behind our old church. It was just a one-room school at first, but quite soon grew into two rooms. We could only hold classes in this facility for a limited number of years, as school buildings were governed by state laws. We definitely had to make plans to build a new school. It was contracted out to one of our own faithful members, Lubert Hop, which made it all a little more possible. Everybody pitched in to help and soon our own school was built.

When the enrollment began for South Olive Christian, we along with some others had to take our children out of the public school where they had always gone. It wasn't easy, because our public school was well thought of in those days. Our own cousin Endine was teacher of our children and it wasn't easy to take them out and send them to our new school at church. Serving on the Christian School Board made this all the more necessary. Marlan was in the fourth grade and Nancy was enrolled in the second grade. We had car pools in those days. Bob and Jack were just in the beginners and first grade.

South Olive Christian was encouraged by other churches in the neighborhood and so our enrollment grew. It was very important for me, as I had attended Holland Christian and graduated because of my own parents' convictions. I felt the importance of our baptismal promise to God in that. God's covenant with Abraham was an everlasting covenant and I also promised the congregation that I would do this to the best of my ability and above all to God whom we confessed and loved with all our hearts. This does not mean we would take care of just our own children, but all of God's covenant children. That's Gospel truth. *Read and believe.*

Roger reading to his kids, Dave and Ellen

My brother Rog and I farmed as Nienhuis Bros. for seven years, and as time went on our family responsibilities increased. Money always seemed scarce, so we decided to do some moonlighting by going to work in the factory again, back to good old Campbell, Wyant & Cannon in Muskegon. Working there made our partnership rather difficult. We put in long days and finally in 1953 decided to separate. Our families were growing and it was time for us to go our separate ways. The question was: who would get what? At that time, we had four different farms to decide on, and as I was the oldest, I decided to take the odd places or other farms, rather than the homestead. Rog and Glad were living on the homestead, so they decided to take that place and Dot and I settled for the rest. There were twenty-six acres out in Harlem four miles away and forty acres of ryeland in hills or wilderness in which trees were planted.[83] We divided all this up at the time.

We became adjusted to the new arrangements. Rog led his farm men and I had mine. We continued to work at CWC together and rode in a car pool along with our brother Clifford, who had worked at the foundry ever since moving to his new farm.

It was in December of that same year, 1953, that Rog and Glad decided to go to the stock show in Chicago, which was a yearly thing in those days. I had gone a year earlier with my older brother El. Rog and Glad decided to go with our nephew, Marvin Dale Nienhuis, and his fiancée Lois Haverdink.

The night before they left, Rog came over and asked me to tell his foreman at CWC that he wouldn't be in the next day. Those were the last words I had with him.

We went to work as always the next day and it was about ten o'clock that brother Clifford came up to me on the job and said, "Drop everything. We got to hurry home." Rog and Glad had had an awful accident and there was little hope for any survivors. A drunken driver had overshot a curve just outside of South Haven and hit them in a head-on collision. It was on Dead Man's Curve, as it was known in those days.

Rog and Glad were in the back seat. Brother Rog got thrown out and was crushed between the two cars as they collided. His wife Gladys was unconscious with serious bodily injuries. Cars were soon gathering at the scene and people were trying to help. Ambulances were coming from all over. An unknown nurse came to Rog's rescue as she kept the blood from choking him. The very gruesome tale was told in the South Haven newspaper.

Brother Rog was hurt the worst. His wife Gladys had a broken pelvis and a skull fracture and Marv's leg was broken along with a serious injury to his thigh. It was a question as to whether they could save his leg or not. Five pounds of flesh was torn out of the upper part of his thigh. Lois had a smashed ankle that isn't ever going to be right, even to this day some fifty years later.

Our mother Nell was staying at our sister Ada and her husband Abe's place while Ada taught in Pine Creek school. Mother always listened to the radio in the morning as the hourly news came on. Before anybody heard anything, she heard that there was an awful accident in South Haven and that there were Nienhuises involved. Of course, knowing that Marv and Rog with their wives were going to the stock show in Chicago set her thinking.

Shortly after, she got a call that we were all going to South Haven in one car. I believe Abe and Ada drove Mother and I and Cliff and Geneva to the hospital. I remember Cliff asking directions at a service station and they remarked that an awful accident had taken place that morning and all were dead. We already knew that wasn't true.

When we got to the hospital, all were living but in very serious condition. We stayed by Rog's bedside night and day as his body was deteriorating. When I turned him over in bed, the sharp bones broken in his back pierced my hand. After an anxious three weeks of praying and hoping, Rog passed away leaving a dear wife in the hospital who couldn't even attend her own husband's funeral.

I was told that when the death was announced on Christmas Morning in our South Olive Christian Reformed Church, everybody was shocked and it made the joyous Christmas Day a sad one for all the family and friends. Three precious children were left, along with a mother who had to go it alone from that time on even to this day, but God filled the emptiness with his Holy Spirit.

The children are all married now and have grown-up children of their own. Roger's wife Gladys never remarried and has some health problems now.

My mother never left the hospital as long as Rog lived. She was by his bedside day and night for three weeks. After his passing, she stayed with Gladys for a number of years.

Gladys stayed in the hospital for at least six weeks for her injuries. Marv not quite that long.

Roger's funeral was held at South Olive Christian Reformed Church. It was held without Gladys, Marv and Lois. In the same hospital, the driver of the other car was also hospitalized and in bad shape. His cursing and swearing was so bad they had to put him on the third floor so it couldn't be heard all over the hospital. He had been driving while drunk after an all-night bender, overshot Dead Man's Curve and caused that awful accident.

The funeral was audiotaped, so Pastor Heyboer and our family went to the bedside of Gladys and all were in one room, along with our closest relatives, and played the tape for her. It was a very sad occasion.

After some six weeks, she returned home and of course there were doctor bills and funeral expenses, all paid by insurance. The accused driver who caused the accident was insured with Lloyds of London so everything got paid.

Well, this too did pass. Our family life changed a whole lot after that. Our oldest boy Marlan, who was twelve at the time, had an awful time adjusting to the fact that his Uncle Rog wasn't around anymore. He almost lived over there with Rog and Gladys, because they were involved in so much machine work together.

Haying at the Tyler Street farm. Probably Marlan on tractor, Bub up top with kids.

From that time on, he worked with me more, as my work load doubled after that.

It was at this time I had to make up my mind to buy out Roger's share of the tools, and that we did. With that expense, that year got to be meager fare. It was just plain tough going. I decided to look for work somewhere other than CWC. The next fall, in 1954, after applying for work a number of places, I succeeded in getting a job at Hart & Cooley in Holland. They were a major company, making heating ducts, registers, filters and other heating and cooling equipment.

It was the month of August that I began working, and I got laid off some six different times before I could apply myself in a way both beneficial for the company and myself, finally landing the right job in the supervisor's station. From that time on, farming became a hobby and a paycheck at the end of the week was an end to our meager fare. My trips to work were close to home, too, compared to CWC, some fifty miles closer round trip, and that in itself was well worth the change.

Through all of these changes, there was a lot of hardship. Dot and I lost so much through the partnership agreement with Nienhuis Bros., and so many changes were necessary.

Marlan helped a lot. At this time, our children were all attending the Christian school and I was deeply involved on the first school board.

It was decided because of financial difficulties that it was necessary for my dear wife to leave her family responsibilities and see if she could find a job. *The Holland Evening Sentinel* listed a job at the Model Laundry in downtown Holland, not far from where she had lived growing up, and she applied and got the job.

So now we had another problem: we needed a babysitter. When the wife, Dot, made the decision to work, I approached my dear old mother and found out she was willing to babysit our youngest, Brian, who was just three years old at the time. Karen was in third or fourth grade at the time. So Mother once again had some family responsibilities and she seemed to appreciate it. She was a wonderful influence on our growing family at the time, and Brian soon got used to that.

Sister-in-law Gladys and her family could get along without Mother, so she spent her days with us and walked back home to Gladys's at night. She would walk both ways, and said she'd do that as long as she could as it was so good for her. This all worked out real well.

It was during this time that I was involved with Sunday School, as I was the superintendent for some ten years. I served while Rev. Heyboer and Dr. Theodore Minnema were our pastors. I enjoyed being involved in that way. Our family was all attending, and that just made it all so worthwhile. We always had our regular teachers' meeting on Friday nights. There was so much meaningfulness and togetherness in our own little get-togethers with the pastor.

It was around this time that I experienced something that I had to live with the rest of my life: I had an injury on the left side of my chin which I received while cranking the hay baler engine. It was slow to heal and when it did, my beard disappeared around the injury and continued to disappear over the left side of my face. I got quite concerned about this and surely wasn't looking forward to losing all my hair.

I went to see our Doctor VandenBerg.[84] He did say that it was rare, but that there was a great possibility that I would lose all my hair. He said it would be something that would surely test our love at home! He recommended applying cyanide to the bald area, which he did without much success.[85] I received many recommendations but no success with any. I became slick bald and stayed that way. My whole body completely rejected hair, as it was explained to me. It was very traumatic at first. I was made the laughing stock of many, and when I went to the barber shop for the last time it was all over. This happened some fifty years ago, and at that time it was suggested to me that fifty years in the future I wouldn't be

100

alone, as many would be shaving their heads by then. I'm finding that to be more true now.

When I started as superintendent of the Sunday School, we changed the school time from after the two o'clock service to after the morning service. When the use of a Dutch service was discontinued and all became English, things started to change in our traditional habits. The elders and deacons always sat together in the front of church and, of course, when the pastor was through with the service it had to meet the approval of the consistory so the pastor shook hands with all of them.

With my wife working and me doing better at Hart & Cooley, we decided to finally do the first remodel on our farmhouse. Our house was too small for our big family of eight people – nine, including my mother when she was there. The kitchen was very small. We still had the outside toilet and some modernizing had to take place.

Hubert Hop, the contractor in our neighborhood, was approached and he made us an offer. We accepted and construction began. It was 1954.[86] We dug out the old Michigan cellar or crawl space on the west side with the tractor and scoop and banked the sand on the driveway between the house and the barn. Marlan was in eighth grade and the younger ones all helped. My brother-in-law Ray Boeskool helped me put a new cement wall and floor under the west side of the house. I then called on a friend to help put in a new furnace and heating runs and it was all done as cheap as possible. Chuck Boersma, neighbor of Hank and Hon, offered to help. He did that kind of work.

At Christmas Time it was all finished. We had a nice, large kitchen and a new basement furnace to keep us warm. We had lots of wood to burn so that kept us warm for the rest of the winter.

We had all my brothers and sisters over on Christmas for a house warming. This was the beginning of changes and there were many more to follow as the family grew and continued to help.

The farming at that time was limited to raising caponettes, as they were known then. Our barn was fixed so that we could have two floors of fast-growing chickens or caponettes. Those chicks were given shots and they grew to six pounds in a couple of months,[87] and it was a good money making thing for us until, after a couple of years, that procedure was outlawed. It turned out that sterilization of the birds caused health problems in people.

We always grew pickles in the summertime, and now the boys and family could help so much that we decided to go into it big. We planted twenty acres of pickles for Heinz. We were able to get Mexican nationals to live all season on our farm, in housing which Heinz furnished. They were excellent pickers. Each had their own row and made sure that the pickles were picked when they were small, which brought the most money. The poor pickers would be influenced to pick better by the better pickers.

When television became a reality, it was not too well thought of and wasn't expected to be in the home of a Christian because of its worldly implications. But it was such an attraction, and for younger people especially. It wasn't long and the more well-to-do people were buying them and tried to keep it a secret at first by keeping the large aerials off the house. Rabbit ears didn't produce the best pictures but it kept them from getting in trouble in the church.

My brother El had one long before we could afford one. We were always welcome there on Friday night after we went to his store to get our week's supply of groceries. The kids were just thrilled to see the wrestling and all kinds of other humorous shows. This went on for a couple years. As the family grew, my dear wife decided to join a Christmas Club at the bank and save for a TV. We bought a Crosley brand TV and that was really swell: all that entertainment right in your own home. Over time, it got to be an accepted thing. Of course, there was no such thing as color television then, it was all black and white. I especially remember some of the first television shows. Wrestling and sports were really

The Tyler Street farm from the air in the late-1960s or possibly '70s, showing the housing provided by Heinz for the farm laborers from Mexico.

swell, as were entertainment such as "My Friend Irma" and Jackie Gleason and of course all the news. We watched "The Today Show" on NBC, with host Jack Lescoulie[88] and so many who have long since passed on.

We avoided all programs that were worldly, especially on Sundays. But there were some real nice religious programs such as "This is the Life" and singing that we could really appreciate. As time went on, everybody had TV.

I recall we had some unusually warm weather on the first of April. I believe it was 1956. This particular thing happened right at the time that Dot my dear wife decided to start working. I remember coming out of the shop at Hart & Cooley and the temperature was above eighty degrees. I remember talking as I walked out about how some bad weather could be expected.

I was driving home that night with the wife from the car pool we had in those days and almost had a head-on collision with a Sheriff's deputy. I was riding on the wrong side of the road to make a turn left down our road. I didn't see him coming because I was distracted by an article in the *Holland Sentinel* that Dot was referring to. Realizing the consequences, I stepped on it and managed to get through the spring-thaw mud holes in Tyler Street, which was a dirt road. In the meantime, he turned around in the neighbor's yard and came after me. I watched his approach to the biggest mud hole and he, to my good fortune, decided to turn around. So that bad mud hole saved me a little money, which we didn't have too much of in those days.

I remember it was that sometime later in the day while I doing chores that the rumbling started. The sky in the west got real dark and Karen who was quite young at the time asked me if I thought we were going to have a bad storm. We all got quite concerned and headed for the basement on the west side of our old house. The storm came over very fast and a lot of wind and rain followed. Our electricity went off as it did quite often in those days. Our electricity, Ottawa & Allegan, O&A, was a pain in the neck the first ten years.

We did not have the worst of that storm, as we were informed later that a terrible destructive tornado went through Hudsonville. A lot of lives were lost and there was considerable property damage. The next day we went to see the damage, and it was unbelievable. There were houses completely demolished and others moved off their foundations.

We had some good years, with Dot and I working along with all the family cooperation, so we decided to take advantage of the Farmers Home Administration loans that the government was offering to farmers at that time and remodel the house again, as we still needed more room.

In order to do this, we were advised to see a certain Mr. Hansen who was working for the government at that time. His office was located in Grand Rapids. It was nice visiting him and getting a lay of the land.

His recommendation was to build new, but we wanted to borrow no more than $10,000 and we believed that we could remodel our old house quite well with that amount of money. The benefit of the FmHA loan was low interest payments.

In order for this remodeling to become a reality, we had to move out once more and live in the upstairs apartment at the homestead again. Of course, all this moving was done on our own with tractor and trailer.

We secured a contractor by the name of Rich Wynn, who had built some beautiful homes in the neighborhood. I liked his work and it was approved by Farmers Home Administration loan officers.

So the first thing we had to do is take off the north side of the old farmhouse. This was quite a task. Our high school boys and a friend did all of that while I was working. This was done in the summer of 1960, and in August that construction began. Our boys helped in every possible way to keep the cost down. When it was

105

finished, our cost was kept down to $7,000. We figured that the rest of the money we borrowed could be used to buy necessities such as carpet and other furnishings.

This got to be a traumatic situation. Our contractor Rich Wynn was called into the FmHA office and was advised that the ten thousand was to be for building only. So the three thousand saved was divided by our contractor and Hansen. So we just gave them all that help for nothing and there was no way for me to correct that situation. It was a very disgusting situation at the time.

But we lived through it. We managed to get our new home furnished and it was just swell to get back in the beautiful new addition with lots of room. We all were so thankful.

Things began to flourish more or less after that. I secured some nice promotions at Hart & Cooley and got to be the night shift foreman on the pipeline and press room. This doubled my income and gave us something for our future.

We had many experiences while the family was growing into maturity, and one of those was a night I shall never forget. We had visited with Dot's sister and her husband, Hank and Hon, as they were known. Their family was much like ours, with equally as many children. Our families grew up together.

On this occasion, we were coming home from their place on a Friday night. It was a very foggy night in October 1960. We got home and went to bed and I remember we were awakened by our collie dog whining and barking. He was a very sensitive and also a pretty dog called Ranger. It was a dark rainy night and the dog did a lot of howling in a mournful way.

Early the next morning, we were awakened by the phone ringing on the party line. The wife lifted the receiver and listened; something terrible had happened.

A small private plane had sent out a distress call to the Holland Airport. They were lost because of the inclimate weather and needed to land. The airport wasn't lit up, so they tried to get as many cars together as they could to park along the runway and light it, but to no avail. By the time they all got together, the plane had disappeared into the dark, foggy night and continued on its lost course.

It was the next morning when our neighbor went to the barn to do chores that he noticed a pile of twisted metal laying on the other side of his straw stack. While walking over to see what it was, he came upon a body of a young soldier boy whose identification was from Bay City, Michigan. He was a star football player we found out later.

I was over there soon after. The wreckage was an airplane rolled up into a large ball. It knocked the top off the straw stack and crashed. Getting closer to the wreckage, we saw bodies hanging from the fuselage. There were four more bodies, all from the same area going home on a weekend pass. They checked out of Fort Hood, Texas, and were going to spend the weekend home in Bay City.

There was a billfold laying on the ground which we picked up to get the identification. The ambulances were called from Holland mainly just to pick up the dead. It was a very gruesome task before breakfast in the morning. I did help place them in a panel truck, all four of them side by side. Something I will never forget. Seeing the pictures of those loved ones in the billfold was more than you could take. It was so *very sad*.

Shortly after the bodies were removed, people started coming and it was a continual stream of cars that day and the next.

Our South Olive Christian school progressed and enrollment increased. We had built that new school in the early 1950s, and with athletics encouraged at the school we just had to add a gymnasium. This was a very good addition. It was used almost every night by people having reunions and programs besides all the games that were held in athletic competition.

Our oldest son Marlan was one of the first ones to graduate from South Olive Christian along with Nancy, who graduated a couple years later. After attending our church school, all the children went on to Holland Christian High School. Bob, Jack, Karen and Brian soon followed.

Mother and I had to keep our nose to the grindstone to pay all the bills, along with the children picking up jobs here and there all to help us along. So many of these things could be done because my dear mother Nellie was with us and also helped all she could.

It was at this time that Bob had a lot of stomach problems. Doctor John Yff, our doctor in Zeeland, diagnosed his problem as duodenal ulcers. All kinds of dieting became necessary, but the pain persisted. Finally, we believed along with the doctor that an operation was necessary, thinking it might be appendicitis. He removed his appendix and also severed a nerve to his stomach all at the same time and believed he took care of his problem. To this day, he has had very little pains of that kind again.

Marlan had graduated from Holland Christian High School a couple years before[89] and went right into the work world. He decided to take a job working for Vern Schaap, who at that time was in the landscaping business. He was working there while Bob was convalescing in Zeeland Hospital. One night while we were coming home from seeing Bob in the hospital, we went through North Holland where there was fog on the road and it was very slippery. I remember saying that there was a truck upside down in the field. Nobody was around, so we just went on home and found out later that our boy Marlan was the driver of that truck and narrowly escaped serious injury. He managed to get the window open and climbed out through the window to get away from the truck, as the smell of gas was strong and he feared it might burst into flames.

Marlan spent a lot of time working for Vern Schaap. It was also at a time when the military was drafting young men again. All available young men over eighteen were required to put two years in the service unless they were in the National Guard.

Marlan tried to get into the Guards but was informed that he already was on draft call,[90] so he knew at that time he would be in the military for two years.

It wasn't long after that that Dot's dad became sick. His health started deteriorating. He developed serious heart problems and was hospitalized. He went in and out of the hospital, until one Saturday afternoon we all were called to the hospital to see him breathe his last. The Father Warner[91] was at his bedside while he died. I remember him reciting the 23rd Psalm while he held his hand and said goodbye. A few days later, the funeral. All the family were present except Marlan, who was gone to Indiana to pick up some heavy equipment for Vern Schaap.[92]

Nancy graduated from high school in 1962. Her first year was spent going to Grand Rapids Junior College to begin a career in nursing, but before she finished her first year she decided to get married.

She was going with Bruce Kuipers and he was in the service and after a lot of long distance phone calls and meetings they decided to marry and live on base. It was a hard time for us, because we missed her so. She went so far from home. At that time, Bruce was stationed in Everett, Washington. In the fall of 1963, Nancy became Mrs. Bruce Kuipers, at our house. The reception was held in the basement or fellowship room of the old church and that same night she said goodbye to us and she was on her way to Everett, Washington with her new husband. There were tears shed and a lot of loneliness until the letters started to come and phone calls came after their arrival. Their trip through the North Country on their way back to Everett was also their Honeymoon.

Bruce was in the Air Force and worked with the Civilian Service as a carpenter and became very good friends with Roy and Vesta Sutter. Roy was involved in Air Force carpentry, as the air base was located near the largest factory in the world at that time, The Boeing Company.

In the living room at the homestead at 124th and Tyler, about 1958:
(clockwise) Nancy, Dot, Bub, Marlan, Bob, Jack, Brian, Karen.

110

Our first grandson was born there about a year later, and of course that made us Grandpa and Grandma. I remember getting the call and how thrilled we all were.

It was only a few months after that an emergency arose and Bruce and Nancy had to come home for a couple weeks. Bruce's brother's wife died of a very serious kidney ailment.[93] Bruce's brother Ron was working for the C.I.A., an intelligence agency. It was so sad, such a young mother taken from her family.

But for us it was quite an excitement, because we were going to see our first grandchild, Jeffery Dean, for the first time. I remember we had put a lot of our old furniture upstairs in the barn and that's where we found the old high chairs and other children's playthings. So we got those back down for Jeffrey. It was so nice to have them over, but it was such a let-down feeling when they left.

After a couple years, we decided to go see them at Christmas Time. Nancy had been over with Jeffrey, who was just a baby the year before, and so we decided to go there the next Christmas.

We thought we would look into going by train. So Mother Dot checked into it and made the proper arrangements and we were off to Everett, Washington. What a swell trip it was. Neither one of us had ever rode on a train before. Brian, who was twelve, and Karen, who was old enough to have a boyfriend, went along. How nice it was to be with them for a while. We spent the whole Christmas vacation there. Jeffrey Dean was a couple years old and of course was the center of attention.

A lot of the homes in the Everett area are built on the side of mountains. Mt. Baker and Mt. Rainier could be seen on clear days. Jeffrey was walking and talking. The weather was around fifty degrees and damp all the time we were there. They had a lot of flooding while we were there. When we went home, we had to be bused to Spokane, Washington where we boarded the train for home. We had a rather exciting time going home: as we neared Chicago, there was a long hold up for a couple hours and we were late getting into Chicago and had to wait for the next train, which they called the mud train or cattle train. It being Old Year's Night,[94] a little too much alcohol had been consumed by some on the train and I was a little afraid that someone was going to be shoved out the doors while the train was moving. An experience I'll never forget. Anyway, when we got to Holland about four o'clock that next morning, the boys were waiting for us and had been waiting there from 6 p.m. the night before.

My mother stayed with us for quite a few years. She was sure a good influence. She reminded us quite often that those days were the best days of our lives, when the striving was the toughest.

It was in 1963, while Karen and Brian were still in grade school, that Mother decided to spend Christmas vacation with my sister Gladys and her husband Dave Van Vliet in Grand Rapids.

She had a nice time with them and was glad to back with us again, but for some reason or other she didn't act the same. She couldn't converse as she did before. We were living upstairs at the time while our old house was being remodeled again, so she was close to help if she needed it.

So Dot and I went to work as usual and coming home that night, Uncle Harry and Aunt Edith had taken Mother to the doctor and found out that she was suffering mini strokes. Not much could be done for her, apparently, and her condition continued to deteriorate to the extent that she couldn't walk or talk. She was hospitalized for some time and then transferred to a convalescent home in Zeeland. It was for a whole year and a half that she lingered in this old Zeeland hospital home before she had a heart attack and died.

The funeral was held in our South Olive Christian Reformed Church. Dr. Minnema preached the funeral sermon. By that time, the funerals had all changed – no more services in the home. They were all held in the church. My mother, Grandma, was eighty years old when she died.[95] Her influence was missed, but God took her and so we had to go on without her. We made a lot of trips to

Singing around the piano at the Tyler Street farm, about 1960 (front, left to right):
Kathe and Marla Postma, children of Hank and Hon Postma; Nancy, Karen;
(back) Marlan, Marla's neighbor and boyfriend Simon, Dot, Bub.

the convalescent home in that year and a half that she survived and then it was all over.

Marlan was going steady with a girl he had gone to school with. We were thankful for that acquaintance; he had others, but this one impressed us the most. As time went on, we all became quite fond of her. It was a comfort to us to know that he had someone special in his life, especially when he was about to embark on a new adventure in Uncle Sam's outfit.

It was a sad day for us to see him leave, along with so many others as strangers. Linda took him to his destination in Grand Haven, where soldiers from around here always left for camp. She kept his car and all seemed quite right that way.

At that time, I made the move at Hart & Cooley to go on the night shift as a foreman. I took advantage of this, making it more possible to get along without my mother, who was in the nursing home at the time. When I went upstairs, it was a sad feeling making Marlan's bed for the last time. Those were some of the heartbreaks we all have to endure in a lifetime, but that too did pass.

It wasn't long and we received letters from him at different locations. First it was boot camp, with all the tough training that goes into that first stop. After that he entered the regular army and put in his two years, going from place to place and not without a lot of disappointment. Linda meant a lot to him at the time, but it was short-lived.

It was about a half a year that he was in service and was getting along quite well that Linda decided to call it quits and sent him a Dear John letter, as it was called in them days. Linda had an old classmate call on her and he swept her off her feet, and being separated from Marlan made it all the more possible.

Marlan was devastated at first and told us she would bring the car back, and so that was the end of that romance. He was a confessing member of our South Olive Christian Reformed Church at the time. It was disappointing to realize how few people of the church paid any attention to him at all. Nobody seemed to be too sympathetic. There wasn't any Christian encouragement. Everybody seemed to be interested in their own things. The feeling there for him was *cold*.

His days were difficult from then on, but he always wrote and so did we. It wasn't long after that that he met one of the girls around the base who was also in the service. That was when Judy came into the picture. Judy was also enlisted and was an Army WAC at the time he became acquainted with her. It seemed they both had a lot in common, and both met on the rebound. We surely didn't hear much of what was going on, so far from home, and we wondered when we got a letter stating they were marrying. They were going to be home on leave around Thanksgiving Day. We sure were anxious to meet his new bride, not knowing at all who she was other than what he told us, and of course that was all good.

They married Nov 12, 1965 and we had no problem getting acquainted on their visit with us. Judy was welcomed into our family. We loved her and were thankful that Marlan wouldn't be alone from then on.

It was at this time Marlan decided to make the army his career. His two years of enlistment were about done and we were expecting him home. It was then that mother answered the phone and found out that he had other plans. He said that he had made up his mind to go to Officers Candidate School. When he said "OCS," his mother got scared and thought he was going to be sent overseas. So Marlan explained and of course that was a shock, too. Well, this meant twenty years of army. We didn't like it, but this is something he and Judy decided and so it was. So that's when we started to take a lot of trips.

After a few months of tough training, he was to become a second lieutenant, and of course there was a graduation. That was the beginning of many trips to Virginia. He was stationed at Fort Lee and was commissioned there as a second lieutenant. We went there with Karen and Brian, who were just kids then. Karen was in high school, Brian in grade school. We made the trip of some 900 miles all in one day. At that time, there were no speed limits so the average speed on those highways was eighty miles an hour or faster, and cars were made to go one hundred miles an hour. Dot drove through the mountains while I tried to relax in the back seat at eighty miles per hour, but our guardian angel was with us. Cars were still passing at that speed.

It was nice being in Marlan's apartment, but we stayed in one of the motels not far from there. The next day was the big graduation. It was wonderful to be there and we were proud of him as his name was called and pronounced so strangely, but he now was a commissioned officer. This was one of our first trips over there and we made many more after that in the twenty years he was in the army.

His first assignment was a trip overseas. He was stationed in Milan, Italy for a couple of years. It was there that our first grand-daughter was born, Michelle Marie.[96] His tour there was cut short due to the Vietnam War. We received a very nice commendation letter from one of the generals pertaining to his ability and rank, but the letter was preparing us for his transfer to Vietnam for a year.

We were informed by a superior officer that Marlan was outstanding in his Quartermaster rank and was due for a promotion, and of course we as parents were happy to hear that. So we finally got the word that they were coming home.

We were notified by the Grand Rapids airport that their arrival from Milan, Italy would be around six o'clock. We were there in plenty of time. At that time, the airport had a lookout area where we could watch the planes coming and going. This was all so exciting, expecting their plane to arrive and seeing our first grand-daughter. Well, it took a long time: it wasn't until one o'clock the next morning that the plane came in. What a grand reunion! They stayed with us for a whole month while Marlan went to war training school. It was July and August. It was the middle of August

116

that he had to leave for Vietnam, so Judy's father and mother came over for a couple of days to see him off. We had a farewell dinner at Van Raalte's in Zeeland the night before and we saw Marlan off at the Grand Rapids airport with a group of other soldiers. Seeing the plane fly away was a very sad time. Marlan was then in the war.

It was while Karen was in the eighth grade that my wife Dot became sick. She had felt tired for a long time and decided to go to Doctor Yff. Our cousin Marion Nienhuis was secretary there. Marion always played piano for us whenever Dot and I sang, and we sang a lot as a duet in those days in all of the churches. Besides, our family also did a lot of singing together.

Dr. Yff was our family doctor after Dr. VandenBerg's passing. He was a very good doctor. When Mother Dot went to see him, he immediately realized that her condition was serious. She was losing blood and had to have a blood transfusion to gain enough strength for an operation. She had a tumor that had to be removed. The operation was planned and took place at Zeeland Hospital and all went well. Dr. Yff said that it was a tumor as large as a sixteen-inch ball[97] that was removed, and after a couple weeks waiting Marion came over one Saturday morning to tell us that it wasn't cancerous. A hysterectomy was also performed at this time and everything looked and went well.

It was a wonderful, blessed experience taking her home from the hospital and our family was all back together again. God answered our prayers in such a wonderful way. Our daughter Karen took care of everything, getting the groceries and doing all the household chores.

Mom soon went back to work at the Model Laundry again and once again everything was back to normal. Karen took music lessons from Mrs. Jacobsen who lived in the neighborhood, which helped her develop her musical talent. She did real well on the piano and also did a lot of singing in high school and for Youth For Christ groups. They sang on the radio quite often at night on Sundays.

While she was going to high school she started going with Gary Raak, a lad from the neighborhood. Gary was successful in joining the Guards, and it was necessary for him to go to camp for six months. He was sent to Fort Dix, New Jersey, where he became deathly sick with meningitis.

We all were prayerfully concerned. Most of his family along with Karen flew over there to be at his side. The army encouraged this as his condition worsened and Karen along with the others were afraid he wasn't going to make it. Our prayers were answered in a wonderful way. He had a miraculous recovery.

Soon after his recovery he came home with an honorable discharge. They got married quite soon after that, in October 1968,[98] in a church wedding at the South Olive Church, and so another one left the nest.

It was August 8, 1969 that Bob and Marcia Vork were married in South Olive Church. Both grew up in the same surroundings right here in South Olive.

Bob was not able to go to the army because of his health. He was working for Van Eyk heating at the time of their marriage. Quite soon after that, he decided to go back to driving trucks for Bil Mar Foods, where he had worked previously. After their marriage, they lived right here in Olive Center in a small house and then moved from there to North Holland where they bought a home and lived for a number of years.

Once again they moved back to Olive Center and lived in a beautiful place along Pigeon Creek where they have now been most of their married lives. Four beautiful children were born to them in this process of moving back and forth: Stephanie and Katie, who are now married and teachers, and Jennie who is majoring in nursing, and Brent who attends Ferris State College at Big Rapids majoring in tool and die. All are doing exceptionally well, *loving God above all*.

My wife, Dot, worked from eight to five o'clock and a half-day on Saturdays. One Saturday morning, April 11, 1970,[99] as she was riding to work down the old Beeline Road, she came to the crossing at Old US 31, stopped, and did not see an approaching car. She started up again and drove right into the path of another car going north. He hit her in the left front corner. Her vision was obscured due to the visor they had on cars in those days.

Dot wasn't hurt as bad as the passenger in the other car. So she ran to a nearby home and called the police and ambulance. After all that was taken care of, a State Police trooper took her home. I had just gotten up for breakfast, as I was working nights. It scared me terribly and quite soon found out that Dot was hurt, also. We went to Doctor Yff in Zeeland and found out she had a broken shoulder. It kept her home for a number of weeks, but the injuries suffered in the other car were much worse. The man who was riding in the front hit his head on the top and had a very serious concussion.

We were concerned about Mr. Leonard Mastenbroek, who was hurt the worst. He went to Holland Hospital and they wanted to keep him there for a couple days, but he wanted to go to Kalamazoo, where he lived. But driving home that distance caused his concussion to hemorrhage and he became incoherent before he reached Bronson Hospital, where he died two days after the accident. It shocked us terribly. What could we do, Dot was not able to ride that far with her sore shoulder. Mr. Mastenbroek had not been in perfect health, which hurried his end. We had no idea what was going to happen but we did know that the accident was our fault and patiently waited for them to make the first move.

In April 1970, Dot was arraigned in court on charges of negligent homicide.[100] The wife being at fault made it very difficult for her to drive. We made a good many trips to Ottawa County Circuit Court in Grand Haven and she had her driver's license taken away and then again renewed a couple days later, and so it went back and forth. She attended a good many court sessions.

We heard nothing about her case until some months later we read a notice in the *Holland Evening Sentinel* that Marvin Nienhuis was being sued for $100,000. We were only insured for ten thousand dollars. It was a big shock for me to read in the *Sentinel* when I came home from work at about 1 a.m. that I was being sued, and there was quite a discussion in bed over that. The wife said, "What do they think we are, millionaires?" It was made official quite soon after that by a Sheriff's deputy, who delivered papers for the lawsuit. Wow, what now? All we could do is pray. Very likely we'd have to declare bankruptcy. We were going to lose everything. And that is the way we felt for a couple months.

We finally got the notice for a court hearing and this brought on a lot of added concerns. The first thing we had to do is get a defense lawyer. I did a lot of calling from the shop and finally got a lawyer named Coupe.[101] He spent quite a bit of time with the wife and helped us through the court session.

We finally had an appointment made with the judge before the court session. We were to meet him at nine o'clock. There were some anxious moments, not knowing what was going to happen. I remember waiting outside of the judge's office and a different lawyer approached us and asked us if we were willing to settle for $20,000. If we would do that, then he would present that to the judge and to the Mastenbroeks, and he advised us to do that as it might settle the matter. So that's what we agreed to do, although my dear wife still believed she wasn't that much at fault. So rather reluctantly we left it that way. We were insured for $10,000 so we had to come up with an additional $10,000. All we could do is go to the bank and borrow and that we did, with a promise to pay within a year. We prayed and God answered our prayers and it was paid up within a year and so we just went on from there. It was a *miracle*.

At the time this all happened, we had a trip to Europe planned. Our boy Jack and Sue were living in Bayreuth, Germany at the time, being in the service. Our son Jack was drafted and was sent overseas in just the opposite direction of Marlan. Jack didn't have to go to Vietnam because there could only be one of a family there at a time, so he was stationed in Germany. Jack was sent there after all his training and we took advantage of his being there by taking a real nice trip all over Europe with them and Sue's folks, Mr. and Mrs. Helder.

Jack was drafted before he was married. I remember riding to Grand Haven with Sue to bring him to the place where he was to be inducted. I had been there so many times before to see our loved ones off. What a sad affair. We kept contact by phone. It was a rough time being in boot camp, but he weathered the storm.

It was while he was in the service that he and Sue decided to marry. Shortly after he was through with boot camp, he managed to get a leave for the purpose of getting married. It was a church wedding in Holland's Prospect Park neighborhood and all went well,[102] and soon thereafter he was sent to the European theatre and Sue went there later. Jack and Sue spent two years in Germany. This was the beginning of our travels. It was just swell going there to see them and our trip over Europe included Germany, France, Belgium and the Netherlands. It was our first time going and what a thrill it was.

Sue's parents were instrumental in arranging our trip. This was done through the Dutch Immigrant Society.

I was working nights as a foreman at Hart & Cooley at the time. My wife Dot went to some of their meetings to make arrangements for our trip to the Netherlands and further to Germany. The Helders made the arrangements. They all went together to Grand Rapids to lay out the plans.

It was on a nice June day in 1970[103] that we boarded a bus to Grand Rapids at the Grandville Christian Church, with our final destination being the Detroit airport. This was real exciting for all of us, as it was going to be our first time we traveled by plane. We boarded the plane and left Detroit at 10 p.m. That was the shortest night we ever lived: while flying east across the Atlantic, the sun was coming up when my watch said it was twelve o'clock midnight our time.

We arrived at Schiphol Airport, Amsterdam, Netherlands, at 10 a.m. our time. What a beautiful view of the Netherlands farm lands, all those nice well-plotted fields. Looking down on them is something I shall never forget. We flew KLM. After a short lay-over there, we were on our way to Frankfurt, Germany.

Arriving there, it seemed like some of the tenseness of World War II or at least the Cold War was still evident, and the surround-ing people were all but cordial. It was there that we boarded a German plane, this time Lufthansa, and headed for Bayreuth where Jack and Sue were waiting for us. It was understood that Frankfurt was one of the hardest-hit cities of World War II, and it had already pretty much been repaired. There were many new buildings.

It was a grand reunion in Bayreuth. It was so nice to see them at the airport, and from there it was just a short trip to where they were staying. Everything seemed so different; living conditions were rough for the people yet, due to the war. We were taken to our motel.

We were introduced to Jack and Sue's landlords, the Gossers. They couldn't understand or talk English, so sign language went a long way. They were wonderful people to know and were quite well to do. Their son was able to converse in English, so our trip through Europe was mainly arranged by him. He knew the import-ant things for us to see. Mr. Helder, Jack and the Gossers' son arranged transportation for the trip. We rented a Volkswagen bus and we were on our way to a new adventure.

We went through Austria and saw the Alps. It was there that we drove to Berchtesgaden in Bavaria and what a place to see. We spent some time there. We went up to the Eagle's Nest, Hitler's hangout during the war days. What a place, the view was breath-taking. It was late June and there was snow up there. The wife had her picture taken standing on a snow bank in her summer dress. We saw the Gold Chamber where Hitler spent his time with his mistress, the walls of the building were three feet thick.[104] There were many buildings that we couldn't enter because of debris left over from the bombing that took place there. There were many craters left that haven't been filled in yet. That place was a real tourist attraction and probably still is.

From there we went to see the death camp at Dachau and the gas chambers where thousands of people met their doom. The smell of dead bodies that were incinerated was still evident. Some people could not enter because of that. It was very gruesome, riding down the same road that these poor people rode to their doom.

We traveled through Germany to Belgium and then to France, where we stayed in Fontainebleau, Napoleon's hangout or stronghold. Also a very interesting place with a lot of history. We spent some time in Paris and took a nice boat ride down the Seine River and could see the beautiful Eiffel Tower some 600 feet high. What a structure, built so many years ago. We also saw many interesting things in the Netherlands. I decided to buy a ready-made diamond at a diamond factory in Amsterdam. Our trip came to a conclusion and soon we were on our way back home. It was a grand experience and that really got us started on our world trips.

The following summer, Jack and Sue came home after his tour of duty and were back in civilian life. They rented the schoolhouse by the old South Olive Church and after that they lived in a home vacated by the Timmer girls, who sold their place, farm and all, to Glen VanderZwaag. He rented it to Jack and Sue until Glen got married and lived there. Then Jack and Sue moved upstairs at the Helders, and in the meantime they adopted Matthew and later Jessica and Christopher from far-off Korea.

The following year it was time for Marlan to come home. Dot and I took a trip to Sioux Center, Iowa, to visit with Judy's parents while we waited for Marlan's arrival back from Vietnam. It was a blessed reunion for all of us, and it didn't take their little girl Michelle long to get reacquainted with her dad. Marlan and Judy and Michelle all came to stay with us after our short stay there.

Our prayers were answered in a very wonderful way. Marlan was back home from that awful war and after that he went back to Fort Lee and then went for some learning to University of Nebraska Omaha to further his education in his promotion arrangement.

It was while he was in Fort Lee that a second child was born, Michael Lee, so at that point we had three grandchildren. Marlan was stationed at Fort Hood in Texas for some time after he graduated from the University of Nebraska Omaha.

We were intending to go see them in Temple, Texas, which is near Fort Hood, but the morning before our trip we had to change our plans.

On that morning, we discovered that our youngest, Brian, had experienced a terrible accident. He had been out partying with his friends that night, and we got a call from the hospital that he would like to see us, as he had an accident falling asleep coming home. There was a phone call at about two o'clock in the morning that scared us and we were on our way there expecting the worst. The very car he was driving was parked up against a tree and we went right past it without knowing it. It was a good thing we didn't know it at the time or that would have worried us even more, as it was demolished. It was completely totaled.

We went directly to the Emergency Room and sat there and waited for a report on our boy, praying that it wouldn't be as bad as we thought. Our prayers were answered in a wonderful way: the doctor came down with the x-ray and gave us the good news that there were no broken bones and that all he had were bumps and bruises. Because of his falling asleep the injuries were less severe. He was released from the hospital and we went home together. He spent a bad night but all healed after a couple of days and went well.

We changed our plans and waited for him to feel better and went to Texas a couple days later.

We did go to Marlan and Judy's, who were living in Temple, Texas while he was stationed at Fort Hood. We were so anxious to see the little grandchildren, Michelle and Michael. We had a wonderful time with Marlan and Judy. He spent his furlough with us, and we tripped all over Texas and went into Mexico. We went to Galveston and also went to Houston and saw the Space Center. We took a tour through the giant Astrodome, which at that time was the largest arena under one roof. We went to see the Waco Arms Museum[105] along with a lot of other places.

We made more than one trip to Texas, with no air conditioning in our car in 90-degree temperatures or even hotter. It was extremely strenuous driving, but we lived through it for better or worse.

It was the following spring, quite soon after our visit to Temple, Texas, that Marlan called and said they were having marital problems. We hoped and prayed that they wouldn't break up, but it wasn't long after that we got word from him that Judy up and left for El Paso, Texas with the two precious little ones. She intended to join a lady who had befriended her while they were at Fort Hood.

Marlan was devastated emotionally, having to carry on in the service without her and the children so many miles away. His place was at Fort Hood and that's where his responsibilities were as a Captain in the U.S. Army. He could not leave Fort Hood and so he lived in the barracks there for some time. This was a terrible heart-breaker for Mom and me.

It wasn't long after that he accepted the situation and went on his way, looking for greener pastures. He started dating again and soon let us know that he had met a gal who was divorced and was in like circumstances. Donna was her name, and he was very serious about her. They shared their woes and soon were on their way to matrimony. Everything looked right to us at this time, because we felt sorry for Marlan, who was really hurting. His divorce was soon finalized, due to the fact that Judy had left him. He decided to come home with Donna at the first furlough, at which time he was informed of another overseas tour of duty. He came home with Donna and we made a grand acquaintance. We appreciated the fact that she loved Marlan.

Marlan decided to take a leave, to which he was entitled, and made arrangements for a home wedding right here in our house. It was hard to accept Marlan's coming home without those precious grandchildren and having to meet a new mother and grandchildren, as she had two young children of her own. But we made the acquaintance quite easily and all fell into place, and Marlan now had four children instead of two, which we saw very little of for a number of years. They arrived at the Grand Rapids airport along with Donna's parents who came also for the wedding which was to take place.

Our pastor at the time was Rev. Maas.[106] Marlan was a confessing member of our church and we believed his divorce was based on biblical grounds. Donna got into the arrangement of things and so Marlan went to see our minister, Pastor Maas, and was given the cold shoulder. The consistory of our church and the pastor as well were not ready for this, because of the divorce issue. This was a big turn-off for one who had not broken any rules and had children baptized in our church and had spent so much time away from our church and supposedly loved ones.

It was an aggravation undeserved and got relieved when he found out that all so-called God-loving people weren't that way. He had a good spiritual talk with his cousin, Rog Timmerman.[107] He was a minister at the Middleville Christian Reformed Church. He saw no reason why he couldn't marry them.

That took place right here in our own living room. It was a very nice home wedding. It was an extremely warm afternoon and Marlan was having problems with his blood pressure. It was during the ceremony, after he sang his song to Donna in front of all of us, that he had to sit down as he felt faint and came very close to passing out. The ceremony was held up for a while. He finished the ceremony sitting down. He was kidded about that by his army associates when they heard about it.[108]

After his return to Fort Lee, he was sent to Thailand with the family. He stayed there a year or more and then returned to Fort Lee where was put in charge of army supply. He got to be a major.

He and Donna lived in Coraopolis, Pennsylvania, for a few years until the Defense Dept. decided to make changes.[109] We visited him quite often then and even lived there for a few weeks in the wintertime and took care of the children while the parents had to finish a custody battle in El Paso. The children were in grade school then.

After they left Coraopolis, they moved to Colonial Heights, Virginia and we spent a lot of time with them there also.

It was quite soon after our being back home from our first trip to Temple, Texas, that our youngest, Brian, started going with Marilyn Vork, Marcia's sister. It was the following summer that Brian and Marilyn married.[110] So brothers married sisters. They too were married in South Olive Christian Reformed Church, and then all the children in our family were married.

The whole family on the Tyler Street farm, Spring 1954: (front, left to right) Karen, Jack, Bob; (rear) Nancy, Dorothy, Marlan, Brian, Marvin.

The Next Generation: Farm Memories of the Children of Bub and Dot

A dedication

Mom and Dad's generation has passed, we kids are now the oldest generation. The circle of life goes on. Brother Marlan passed away on June 11, 2020. He was seventy-eight. He is buried at Houston National Cemetery on a beautiful grassy hill overlooking a crystal-blue pond. He served his country honorably for twenty years and retired as Major Marlan L. Nienhuis, so he received a full military funeral. We visited the cemetery a few months later to look for his newly placed gravestone. We searched among the rows of white and there it was. The name Nienhuis stood out among all the other names.

I studied the beautiful marker and my thoughts went back to our beginnings on those dusty country roads in Crisp, Michigan at Grandma and Grandpa Nienhuis's homestead and our farm across the east forty. I thought about us kids playing in the hay mow, the old wheat granary, the milk house water cooler, and Marlan driving the tractor on those acres of hay, corn and pickles. I'm sure he never thought about all he would accomplish in his life. Or that it would take him to so many countries all over the world. Marlan loved to reminisce about the good old days. He left the farm in Michigan for a world of experiences and now he is at rest on a grassy knoll under the Texas sky.

Dad would like it. I can see him smile.

—Nancy Jane Wilson

1941–1963,
My Years on the Farm:
The Good, the Bad, the Memorable
and the Forgettable

Marlan Lee Nienhuis

Here we go through the eyes and the mind of a young witness to some of the events on the farm and life in general at that time.

It all began for me on October 11, 1941. I can't recall anything prior to beginning school. Unlike Dad, who Mom often accused of remembering what occurred prior to his birth. Dad's memory of World War I was often questioned by Mom and others because he was only two years old in 1918.

My first memory is of school, age four, in September of 1946. I turned five in October 1946.

I attended kindergarten at the West Crisp School. We had two rooms: Kindergarten thru 4th in one room and 5th thru 8th in the Big Room. This is the same school Dad and his siblings all attended. My Little Room teacher was Miss Brooks. I thought she was a hundred years old. My only academic memory from that first year was the poem, "Hey diddle diddle, the cat and the fiddle, the cow jumped over the moon."

I thought this was crazy. I knew cows and they certainly would not be jumping over the moon. There were no school busses at this time, so Dad dropped me at school while he was on his milk route in the morning. Transportation was in the old Dodge pickup, a 1930-something model.

Picking up milk from the farmers who were customers was interesting. Milk was kept in cans which were stored in a concrete water tank in what was called the milk house. Water in the tank was first naturally cooled. Refrigerated coolers for these cans arrived on the scene later. Those cans were heavy! Milk went to the Holland Rusk Company factory.

School was okay but farming was my real interest. Uncle Roger, whom we called Uncle Rog, was my hero in this farming effort. Time I could spend with him, doing whatever he did, was *great*.

The story goes that I was around six years old and it was haying time. Uncle Rog said I could drive the tractor pulling the wagon and the hay loader. Dad and Rog needed to deal with the hay coming onto the wagon. All I needed to do was keep the tractor on the windrow of hay. On a hill, the tractor stalled. Uncle Rog yelled, "Start it up again!" and start it I did. I knew exactly what to do, I had seen him do it a hundred times. I always rode with him on the tractor whenever I could. That was the case with most everything.

Before age ten, I was allowed to do almost everything with a tractor – plow, drag, disk, etc. I loved it more than I did school. School grades were okay but I'm sure they could have been better.

In the late 1940s, we still had a team of horses on the old farm on 124th Avenue, the farm we all called "the homestead." They were huge draft horses named Daisy and Doll – we called them Daze and Doll. They were used for pulling wagons, manure spreaders, hay mowers, etc. Dad used them to cultivate corn, pickles, and sugar beets. Uncle Rog was more into the speed you could get with a tractor. I believe they bought their first tractor, a Farmall H, in 1939. It was around into the 1960s.

Grain threshing and harvesting, before the advent of the combine, was a great time of the year for me. All the neighborhood farmers worked together, going from farm to farm with the threshing machine. Lunch was always a large family-style meal prepared by the host farmer of the day or days that the operation was at that location. At the end of the day, there was always lots of soda and beer for the workers. Operations usually ended around four o'clock in the afternoon, as all the farmers had their own home chores to do. The last threshing I remember was at the farm in 1954 or 1955.

The square-baling of hay and straw gained popularity in the late 1940s. Dad and Rog, as the Nienhuis Bros., had one of the few balers in the area and began doing custom hay and straw baling for 10 cents per bale. This was a busy time between June and September. The days were long, weather permitting; the latest I recall working was until midnight.

Uncle Will,[111] Dad's oldest uncle, lived on the farm directly south of the homestead. Dad and Rog rented most of his land for farming. I'm pretty sure Uncle Will was suffering from some form of dementia, but he always wanted to help when he could. In the summer, after the wheat and oats were harvested and bundled, they needed to be shocked. Usually four to six pairs of bundles set upright to make a shock. On one occasion in summer 1946 or '47, while helping to shock wheat, Uncle Will set one shock with at least twenty-five or thirty pairs of bundles. Uncle Rog said to Uncle Will, "You have created the largest shock in Michigan," and just left it at that, no harm done.

In the late 1940s and early '50s, farming equipment not in use was stored in the barn on Mrs. Looman's farm. This was the farm directly north of the homestead on 124th. Our hayloader, grain binder, corn binder, side rake for hay, and grain drill were all stored there. Also in this barn were old carriages, horse buggies and sleighs. I had no idea who they belonged to but they were old.

During those same years, a Christmas gathering of all the aunts, uncles and children would take place in December. The gathering involved the usual eating and gift exchange, and was a real fun time. The celebration would always take place at the homestead and snow would usually cause some problems for the travelers. The road, 124th between the homestead and Tyler, usually caused the most trouble. Uncle Rog was always more than able to clear and assist anyone through this area with the trusty tractor without a problem. As usual, I was at his side so as not to miss out on the action.

Brother Jack was born on a cold winter day, February 1947. After numerous days in the hospital, he and Mom returned in an ambulance. The snow was deep.

Sister Karen's birth occurred while were living upstairs at the homestead. A neighbor, Noreen Weener, kept an eye on us at that location while Mom was in the hospital.

Barn remodeling on the Tyler Street farm took place around 1950. Concrete floors were put in along with a new milking system. I saw this as the first step in the Nienhuis Brothers' move to a bigger operation. Capacity for milking increased as the number of dairy cows increased. During this time, a new tractor and attached equipment was purchased, continuing the expansion thru the early 1950s.

At this time, Uncle Rog and Aunt Gladys decided to remodel the homestead. The beautiful old Victorian house was ruined. In its place came a typical 1950s-era-styled house. It could have been updated without totally destroying its character forever. It all made me sad at the time and does to this day.

In July of 1950, at age nine, I had a mishap while at the farm. Nancy, Bob and Jack were playing in some sand in front of the barn. I seemed to find some pleasure in riding my bicycle through their creations and destroying them. This created a screaming furor on Nancy's part. Dad came out of the barn and warned me not to do it again or else I'd know what he meant. I did it again and with some results. Dad came out of the barn after me and knew what he had in mind. I dropped my bike and chose to run for it down the driveway toward the road. Seeing that Dad was gaining on me, I took a sharp left and fell down. Dad's foot came down on my leg and you guessed it, SNAP. I heard it but didn't feel it. I tried to get up to continue my escape. I couldn't, I had a leg problem. Broken between the knee and ankle. Accidental discipline was administered, and Dad said he was sure the punishment did exceed the crime. My hero Uncle Rog was not happy. My leg was in a cast from the knee down for about six months. I remember walking home from school on crutches that fall. I didn't really think about it.

In the late 1940s and early '50s, a peddler truck traveled the neighborhoods. It carried a mini grocery store full of items such as sugar, salt, dry cereals, flour, a few sundries like needle and thread, and some candy. Grandma Nell was the buyer at the homestead. The truck was owned and operated by John Redder, who owned the Olive Center Grocery Store.

The Sunbeam Bread truck also made a weekly visit. It was a '50s model Chevrolet panel truck outfitted to display all the bread and goodies inside. Besides bread, it had sweet pastries and snacks like Ho-Ho and Twinkie-type stuff.

Cousin Peter Van Vliet was a frequent homestead visitor in the 1940s and '50s. He traveled from Grand Rapids on his Wizard motorbike.

In the late 1940s, cousin Arthur Nienhuis[112] spent time at the homestead. He and I are just one month apart in age. During one of these summertime visits, he and I got into some trouble with Aunt Gladys. The incident involved Art and I knocking one of the tire rim flower pots off the porch. Lord, you would have thought it was the end of the world. Just kids playing around, we were probably eight years old at the time.

The farm operation also owned forty acres of property in Harlem. In the late 1940s and '50s, this land was used primarily for pasture for the Holstein heifers. When the two-lane divided highway, US 31, was built in 1950, the western twenty acres were sold to the state for right-of-way. An additional five-acre plot was leased to the highway construction company, Cannoni & Sons, for the concrete batch plant.[113] I believe the water pond they dug remains to this day.

Also adjacent to this property was the H.J. Heinz pickle factory and the Harlem Farmers Co-op. The co-op ultimately was purchased by Bil Mar turkey farms and Brother Bob spent a career there as a manager of the mill.

Cousin Marv spent a lot of time at the homestead during the 1940s thru 1950. He did a lot of farming assistance, particularly during the summer months. He had a beautiful Cushman motor scooter he used to travel from Holland. He followed up with a beautiful 1951 Ford Victoria two-door hardtop. It was dressed up in classic cruiser style. It was this vehicle that everyone was in at the time of a deadly crash in December 1953.

That December, on a weekend trip to the Chicago Stock Show, Uncle Rog, Aunt Gladys, cousin Marv and his girlfriend Lois Haverdink were involved in a head-on crash on old US 31 in South Haven that changed lives forever. Uncle Rog was thrown from the vehicle and suffered a broken neck. To my knowledge, he never regained consciousness. On Christmas Eve 1953, he passed away. At twelve years of age, it seemed my world had come to an end. My hero was gone. It did come to an end as it had existed. What would I do now?

The farming continued, but it wasn't the same, that's for sure. Poor Dad, I think what he did to keep things going was more for me than being a good business decision. He purchased the hay baler and made some sort of arrangement with Aunt Gladys concerning the ending of Nienhuis Bros. During the late 1940s and early '50s, Dad and Rog both spent time working at factories outside of farming, and that was Dad's focus after Rog was gone.

During the 1951–53 period, Dad on Sundays would write in his diary. He also would write letters to area soldiers stationed in Korea and elsewhere.

In 1955, high school began for me. Dad was working outside the farm. Chores needed to be done. I started at around 4 a.m. and had to be ready to go to school at 7:30. This went on for some time, how long I don't remember. This also was the time the Tyler Street farmhouse received its first remodeling. This brought indoor plumbing and made obsolete the outdoor toilet. A great day that was, for sure!

After graduating from high school in 1959, I was asked to put some of my farming experience to work if I chose to. Dad's cousin Ethel Kraai and her husband had a farm north of Zeeland on State Street. They had a four-month trip planned to Alaska. I accepted the job and worked five days a week from 5 a.m. until mid- to late-afternoon. My main task was morning milking. They had around thirty dairy cows. Their son Terry took care of all evening and weekend chores and milkings. I enjoyed it a lot. He had nice equipment to work with. My favorite was a new Allis Chalmers tractor with a three-bottom plow. It was awesome.

This was my last experience with farming. Bob and Jack took over what was going on back home. I moved to working at a car dealer and an excavation contractor until December 1963. We all know what happened then: Uncle Sam called and I never returned except to visit.

Farm, Faith and Family
Woven with Music

Nancy Jane Wilson

My memories go back and forth between the farm on 124th Avenue owned by my Grandpa Martin and Grandma Nell Nienhuis, which we called "the homestead," and the Tyler Street farm. Grandpa and Grandma's farm was just across the long field from the Tyler Street farm and we could always see it. Memories are confused in my mind as to which farm it was where they were experienced and at what time of my life. I grew up on both farms and they both felt like home.

Farm Life

I was born while we lived at the Tyler Street farm, as were Marlan, Bob and Jack. I have pictures of Marlan, me and Bob there. We were all dressed up for church. At the time, our ages must have been around six, four and two. Jack must have been around a year old. Memories of those first years are very vague, except for one: I was probably around four years old, and I remember playing with Marlan and Bob near the barn where the cow tank stood. It was on the east side of the barn toward the end nearest the house. The water in the cow tank was very tempting and I couldn't keep my hands out of it. I fell in. Dad heard my screams and pulled me out. I didn't get any sympathy. I specifically remember him telling me as I was dripping wet to go to the house to see Mom. After all these years, I still believe it was Marlan who pushed me in!

Many of my earliest childhood memories are from the homestead. I was around five years old when we moved from Tyler Street to the second-floor apartment at the homestead. It was

1949. The move was necessitated by a pending remodel to the Tyler Street farmhouse; a new kitchen and indoor plumbing was planned. After we'd lived at the homestead a while, however, the remodel was put on hold and a newlywed couple from our church, Howard and Noreen Weener, rented the Tyler Street house. So, we ended up staying at the homestead for a few years.

That house was very big and it was always full of people, but the atmosphere had changed since Mom and Dad married: Grandpa Nienhuis had passed away a few years before I was born, and Grandma continued to live downstairs with Uncle Roger and Aunt Gladys. The large upstairs had been remodeled into an apartment where we would live off and on throughout my growing-up years. That was not uncommon in those days, as times were hard and young married couples needed places to live: I recall that Dad's cousin Chet Schemper and his wife Garry lived upstairs at Uncle Harry and Aunt Edith's home, too.

I have faint memories of being upstairs at the homestead and watching the large stairway being removed and seeing the big black hole to the downstairs living area. The stairway had to move so a new bathroom could be installed. I don't think we were living there at the time but soon thereafter. I liked living there. The apartment was nice and it had a bathroom! The apartment had a big kitchen and dining area and a good-sized living room. There was a small room off the dining area that was our playroom. I remember a lot of coloring on the walls in that playroom! Those marks might still be there.

We went back and forth from the homestead to Tyler Street quite a few times! Back and forth! After a few years, the remodel at Tyler was completed and back we went to a house with indoor plumbing and a bigger kitchen. As we six kids grew older, more room was necessary. In 1960, we moved back to the homestead so a complete remodel of the farmhouse could be done. Dad, Mom and all of us helped wherever we could. We kids painted and stained all the trim. I didn't enjoy that at all, but the new house was beautiful.

Meanwhile, back at the homestead, the farm was full of activity. Dad ran a milk route. He would pick up milk that the farmers put in big milk cans. I can still see Dad lifting those heavy cans full of milk onto the old truck bed. We loved that old Dodge truck with the big headlights on the front. We would saddle ride on them when Dad went back and forth from the homestead to the Tyler St. farm. I remember thinking he was very strong. He had quite a few stops at different farms. He would deliver the milk to the rusk factory that was located in downtown Holland. Sometimes I would ride along with Dad on these milk runs. I remember at one of those deliveries, Dad decided to carry me into the rusk factory to show the ladies his little girl. The ladies were working on a big table rolling out dough and there was flour everywhere. They wanted to pick me up. I can remember not wanting to be full of all that flour.

I loved the fall. It was threshing time. All the men and boys from the family gathered at the homestead and worked long days gathering the wheat, threshing it and filling the granary. Grandma and the ladies prepared food. The milk house cooler was full of O-so grape and orange pop. It wasn't until just a few years ago that I found out there was beer for the men in there too! Fun was had by all!

I have a vivid memory of an incident that happened while I was attending kindergarten at the West Crisp School. It was 1949, and we were living at the homestead at that time. The entry to the school had a very large, heavy front door. All the children were coming back into the schoolhouse after recess and that big heavy door shut on my finger. I can still see all the blood and feel the pain! Our teacher, Mrs. Elenbaas, bandaged me up and called the farm (yes, we had a telephone, it was a big wood phone mounted on the wall. Our phone number was 23F15, one long ring and five short rings) thinking I would want to go home. Dad came to get me in the old pickup. I can remember being very emphatic about not wanting to go home. I wanted to be in school. Dad left me there!

I also remember all the students being given an afternoon snack of canned prunes. I believe the school was given surplus canned goods left over from the war. Not sure why we always got prunes, but I distinctly remember eating prunes. I did not like prunes.

Marlan and I walked the three country miles to West Crisp School. Marlan attended his first three years of school there. I attended there only my kindergarten year, 1949. The next year, the South Olive Christian School was opened and from then on, all of us siblings attended there.

Dad was very instrumental in starting South Olive Christian School. He served on the committee to organize the Christian school. I can remember Dad attending a lot of meetings at church. He was very committed to giving his children a Christian education. Starting a school was quite controversial back then and it divided the church for some time. I believe the decision to form a Christian school was made when the public schools were consolidating and expanding, and it wasn't too long after this that the federal court took the freedom to pray out of the public schools.[114] The South Olive Christian School was formed in 1950 and was held in the chapel attached to the church. As it grew, it was moved to the basement of the church. Dad remained on the school board for many years and served on the building committee for the new school building, which remains today. It was very costly to send us to the Christian school. Mom and Dad went without so they could send all six of us kids to Christian schools until we all graduated from high school.

I have sweet memories of walking with Grandma Nell down Tyler Street to and from the farms. Tyler Street was a gravel road. I can still hear the crunch of the gravel while we walked. I particularly remember walking with Grandma down 124th Avenue to Mrs. Looman's house for tea. Mrs. Looman was very old, and her house was very old.[115] It had a handle water pump by the sink in the kitchen. I explored her bedroom and touched the china water pitcher and basin on her dresser. Mrs. Looman was a midwife and assisted Grandma with the births of some of her children. I am not sure she helped Grandma with Dad's birth, but it is possible.

Most of our growing up happened at the Tyler St. farm. There are so many fond memories there. I have a strong memory of being in the barn with Dad while he milked in the evening. I distinctly remember the back door in the stable being open and looking out the back toward the catalpa tree woods. The trees were in bloom. It must have been spring. I also remember the old radio in the stable; it was a Crosley floor model. It was big. Dad was listening to the news on WHTC.

We loved playing in the catalpa woods and on the old railroad bed. Dad and Grandpa Nienhuis planted the catalpas for fence posts years earlier. There was a lot of water and little islands along the railroad bed that had been formed many years before when the railroad workers scooped out dirt to build up the raised bed for the tracks. Those islands were our little sanctuaries. Mom would make us lunches of soda crackers and peanut butter for picnics on those little islands. We spent a lot of time building tree forts in the trees. The catalpa's spring blooms are white. We knew spring had arrived when the woods was aglow with white blossoms. The catalpa woods still blossoms so beautifully every spring.

I have sweet memories of walking down the railroad bed with Mom and Dad in the spring looking for the wild flower, trillium. They grew in the cool moist areas under the umbrella plants, or what some people call mayapples. The trillium still come up each spring to this day.

There was a lot of activity at the farm, especially in the summer. Dad raised pickles and he hired Mexican migrants to pick the pickles in late summer. Small houses were put on our property along the railroad bed for the migrant families to live in. I can still smell the tortillas cooking. We played with the children while their parents picked the pickles. It was hard work. Bob, Jack and Marlan were asked to pick the pickles too. I had to help make the meals and keep the house clean, but lucky me, I didn't have to pick pickles.

Grandma did, however, ask me to go to the garden and dig potatoes for supper. I had to make sure I didn't pierce the potatoes with the shovel. Digging potatoes is a skill that takes practice to do well. I do recall picking rows and rows of green beans, peeling bushels of apples for applesauce and processing bushels of peaches. Every fall we drove to Fennville to get peaches. It was an outing for us kids.

I would sometimes deliver lunch to Dad, who was plowing the field west of the barn. I was little, but it wasn't a long walk from the house. I remember distinctly what Mom made for his lunch: dried beef and cheese on raisin bread and a thermos of hot coffee.

Faith

Attending church was the center of our life. Every Sunday morning at exactly 9:00 a.m., the custodian of the church, Lawrence VanderZwaag, would ring the church bell to call us to worship. It is still done today. We had two services, morning and evening. I do remember attending Sunday afternoon church in the winter. It was held at 2 p.m. because it was hard for the church members to get to church on those cold and dark winter evenings. In my early years, the church held an afternoon service that was conducted in Dutch. The church was beautifully built; the ceiling tiles were so intricate. The Sunday service sermons were quite boring for us little ones, so we often spent our time counting those beautiful tiles on the ceiling. You can ask any of the kids who attended in those days and they would say the same thing.

In the summer, like clockwork, right before the sermon, the custodian would use a long iron stick to open those beautiful stained glass windows high above the sanctuary to let in some air. I remember it was a big deal for boys to become a teenager in the church, because they could sit in the back of the church with all their friends. Sometimes they would get reprimanded by the dominie – the pastor – for not paying attention to the sermon. I do remember an instance when little brother Brian was not enjoying having to sit still. Dad had to take him out of the sanctuary, and I could hear him crying all the way out in the parking lot!

We were given peppermint candies when we were in church, and they were either pink or white. I always liked the white peppermints. Dad liked white peppermints, too. Mom always had eight peppermints in her purse and they were passed out at the beginning of the sermon: pink for those who liked pink and white for those who liked white. Guess it helped us kids sit still!

Family

We had uncles and aunts who lived within walking distance of the farm. Dad's cousins and aunts also lived within a few miles. Dad loved it that way. Our community *was* a big family; it actually was a very large, extended family. Uncle Clifford and Aunt Geneva lived a mile down 124th Avenue. Grandma's sister and her husband, Uncle Harry and Aunt Edith, lived a half-mile down 124th. Of course, the homestead was a quarter-mile from the Tyler St. farm, and we lived on the homestead with Grandma and Uncle Rog and Aunt Gladys for a number of years. There was always someone stopping by on the farm. In the fall, the uncles and cousins came to help with the threshing. Mom's family, the Van Langeveldes, lived in Holland, in what we considered to be the city. Her sisters and their families came to visit the farm often.

We had family reunions every summer. Family reunions were a big deal in the Nienhuis Family. I remember a reunion held at the Overisel Hall; to me it seemed like a big place, they even had a balcony. We kids sat up there! Along with a lot of food, a program was put together for everyone's entertainment. There would be skits and plays and poetry readings. There were always updates on what was happening in the family, new babies, who graduated from school and went on to college. Grandma's sister, Aunt Nettie, lived in California so the family got updates on what was happening in her life.

And always, we sang. The whole family was full of good singers, and when we were in such a large gathering, we sounded like a beautiful choir!

Over the years, the cousins and their families made many visits back to the farm.

Side note, December 6, 2018: Today I went to the funeral of my cousin Peter Van Vliet. How could I lose a cousin so soon? I learned he was 84 years old. Dad's older sister Gladys married David Van Vliet and moved to Grand Rapids, and they soon had Peter. We loved it when cousin Peter came to visit. I remember him being quite silly, maybe he was a bit like Uncle Roger. I specifically remember Peter playing the piano with his toes. I was maybe six or seven then, Peter maybe a teen. I truly believed he could play the piano with his toes! Recently, brother Bob reminisced about how cousin Peter did magic tricks, like swallowing a knife. We were so amazed at how he could do that! Bob was probably around five years old at the time.

We didn't see Peter's family much after we all went on to college and started families, except for a few family reunions which, in later years, were always held at our farm on Tyler Street. Peter became a doctor and lived an exemplary life. He had four sons. At the funeral, I identified myself as cousin Nancy, of Bub and Dot Nienhuis. They all knew exactly who I was. They remembered Bub and Dot. They remembered the farm.

Whenever I see cousins and the cousins' kids, they all have the same comment: they all remember the farm. That's what the farm was. It was a place that grew memories for everyone.

Uncle Roger

Uncle Rog was the youngest of my dad's brothers, the baby of the family. He was wild and crazy, impromptu and silly. We had so much fun with him. He loved to drive very fast. I can remember specifically one day playing outside and hearing a car rumbling over the old bridge on 124th Avenue. A car was flying down the dirt road and sure enough, here came Uncle Rog roaring into the driveway with a cloud of dust behind him.

Marlan was very close to Uncle Rog. Rog taught Marlan how drive the tractor when he was five years old. Uncle Rog and Dad were running the farm after Grandpa Martin died and they had big plans to expand the farm. But life on the farm changed forever on Dec. 2, 1953: Uncle Rog and Aunt Gladys were in a terrible accident near South Haven on their way to Chicago with my cousin, Marv, and his fiancée Lois. I remember us kids being cared for by different neighbors while Mom and Dad and Grandma went back and forth to the hospital. Uncle Rog died on Christmas Day. It was a Sunday. I can remember crying so hard at the funeral. I can still feel it. It brings tears as I write this. He was only twenty-nine years old. Dad could not run the farm alone. Farming at the homestead ended. Dad concentrated on farming at Tyler Street. From then on, the Tyler St. farm became the center of our lives. Losing Uncle Rog changed everything about the farm. Marlan was never the same.

Music

Music played a major role in our lives. Dad's life growing up was full of music. I remember hearing that Grandpa Martin and Grandpa's brothers sang together in a quartet; Marlan doesn't remember that, so maybe I dreamed it. But the old farmhouse was full of guitars, a mandolin and a piano. They had a beautiful pump organ at the homestead that followed us to the Tyler farm. I loved trying to play it, even though I had a hard time pumping those peddles. Dad was a perfect tenor and Mom a perfect contralto. Mom and Dad sang together as a duet at special occasions and at church services. So it was very common for family gatherings and reunions to include singing hymns.

Dad encouraged all of us kids to sing and learn to play the piano. Once I knew how to play, I was volunteered to play the piano at the family hymn sings. I have sweet memories of our rides home after our Friday night visits to uncles and aunts in town, with all of us singing Sunday School songs together in the car. Dad never had piano lessons, but he learned to play by ear. The only song he could play was his favorite hymn, "What a Friend We Have in Jesus." Our whole family participated in the church choir. On occasion, our family would sing together at the church service. Marlan sang bass; Bob and Jack, Karen and little Brian sang the melody; Mom and I sang alto; and of course Dad sang tenor. As all of us kids learned to harmonize, Bob, Jack and Brian became good baritones and tenors. I loved to sing the alto part. We were pretty good! Dad always had a song to sing. He also was very good at whistling. He was always whistling a tune. Dad and Mom sang in the choir until they were eighty.

Memories dearest to me are of Friday night trips to town for haircuts, groceries and shoes. Someone always needed new shoes. Mom and Dad always saw to it that we kids had good shoes, maybe because Dad's feet had been damaged by not having the right shoes during the Depression. We often stopped to visit Uncle Hank and Aunt Hon and all the cousins. Fridays often found us at Uncle El's and Aunt Henrietta's place to watch boxing on TV. We didn't have a TV, and Mom and Dad loved to watch boxing.

Saturday night was hamburger night! After having meat, potatoes, green beans and applesauce all week, those hamburgers were such a treat. Mom would make homemade hamburger buns, too. Yum, yum!

As we left home to start our own families, it was still tradition to have dinner at Mom and Dad's place on Tyler St. every Sunday. Mom's roast beef and mashed potatoes were the best! And those pies!

In later years, Saturday afternoon coffee was designated to discuss the pig business that Dad, Bob and Jack had started and whatever else was going on at the farm and in the community. Saturdays were also set aside to cut wood for the wood stoves, often on that dangerous old buzz saw run off the wheel of the tractor. Many cords of wood were cut over the years. If we were coming out to visit Mom and Dad on a Saturday, we always made sure we arrived before 3:30 p.m. for Saturday coffee time.

Many memories were made around that kitchen table.

My dad pretty much stopped running his big farm operation after Uncle Rog died. That was in 1953, and I was eight when he died. Dad farmed full-time for probably a couple years after that, but it went downhill pretty fast. By the time I was ten, he was working nights at Hart & Cooley. After that, we just grew pickles. He and Uncle Rog had done some of that together; I guess we just went on growing pickles after Uncle Rog died and all the cows and stuff went away.

We had about ten acres in pickles, just to the west of where the barn is now. We kept on growing pickles because it was pretty profitable. One year, we had an exceptionally good year and I remember Dad saying he made $6,000 that summer, which is equivalent today to about $50,000.

We all worked in the pickles. Us kids did all the hoeing. Along with some neighbor kids, we hoed them two or three times a season, I think. Man, that was a terrible job! It used to kill us. Once we got through the hoeing part, then it was fun. Picking and stuff was more fun. Then we had Mexican nationals come during the summer and they lived in what we called "Mexican coops" that were set up on the old railroad bed; there were three or four of them up there. I think we had about ten to twelve Mexican nationals who lived there. At that time, it was all men, when I was helping with the pickles. Later on, they came as families and they lived in there with their kids and all.

I got to know some of those guys. They tried to teach us Spanish. We would be walking in the field while they were picking pickles, and we would spend an hour or so out there and they would teach us how to count and probably say some naughty words. It was kind of fun. I never learned to speak it, but we all picked up just a few words, like dog, cat, cow. We could count to fifty. Just a few words.

When I graduated from high school, I got a job at Roamer Boat in Holland and that only lasted three months. They made steel-hulled boats covered with fiberglass. I was on the finishing line. As the boats went out the door and were ready to be water tested, I had to go through and inspect all the fiberglass and if there were any nicks or stuff I had to flag them. It was a real gravy job. But they kind of used me there: I replaced a guy who was in the National Guard and he had to go on a two- or three-month training exercise or something. He was going to be gone, so he trained me to do his job and as soon as he got back they fired me.

So I was still living at home and I sat around for about a month and was looking for a job, which was pretty hard to find then. One day this old Dutchman comes to the door and he says that a friend of mine had been laid off at Hart & Cooley, which is kind of ironic, since Dad worked there. My friend got laid off and went to work for Bil Mar, the huge turkey operation run by ol' Marv DeWitt. So this guy worked there for a while and then he got his job back at Hart & Cooley and he told his boss, an old Dutchman, that I was looking for a job. So the old Dutchman come to the door and asked me if I wanted to work at Bil Mar. I said, "Shoot yeah, I'll work." He said, "You be at the plant at four o'clock Monday morning and we're going to load turkeys."

Oh boy, did we load turkeys. Twelve hours straight, and it was all by hand. I did that three days in a row and I was going to quit. I was just dead. The third day we loaded turkeys in the morning, and in the afternoon he took me off that and took me out to the ranges where the turkeys run around, which is out in the open, and he had me move feeders and do stuff with the tractor. I thought it was heaven on earth. I only loaded turkeys a few times after that. The rest of the time I was working with the turkeys on a tractor and all that, and then a year later he made me manager of one half of the kingdom out there, which was about 300,000 turkeys. And he ran the other half. There were a *lot* of turkeys out there.

Anyway, that's how I got started at Bil Mar, which became my career. I was living at home yet and of course Dad was working nights, so I didn't see him hardly ever. Mostly I lived with Mom. And she was working, too, at the laundry. But Grandma Nell was there every day. She walked over from the homestead to our house and took care of us kids. She would make our lunch and do housework. And make sure we did our work. Especially hoeing pickles. Oh boy, she was a pretty tough lady. But she was good, too.

Dad used to raise ducks in the barn on Tyler Street, too. Not just the milking operation. Oh, it seemed to me like we had 5,000 ducks but it might've only been 500. I don't know. I must've been six or seven years old when we had that. They were on the west side of the barn because we had the milk cows on the east side of the barn. I remember Dad would let those ducks out every day, just let them out, and they'd go way out in the field to find the mud holes and us kids would have to go out there and chase them back to the barn. They would go right back, I don't know why, but they would go right back to the barn at night.

We must've had them for a year or two. We used to have a duck egg scale. It was a little thing you could lay an egg in and it would tell you how much it weighed. Maybe they were graded that way. Mom took care of all the eggs. I guess that's why we raised them, for the eggs. I don't know who would ever want a duck egg, but she took care of those. Ducks are terribly messy. I remember that side of the barn was just terrible.

Of course, we also raised caponette chickens. They were given a shot to make them grow or something like that, Dad said, but that must have been done before we got them. We got them as chicks. I think we had about 2,500 of those. They were all running loose. The whole upstairs of the barn and the whole bottom of the barn was all chickens. Oh boy. That was me and Jack's job. We would have to feed them morning and night, and we would go out there early in the morning and feed them and we must have stunk like chickens but then we would go to school. We would go right to school after feeding them, just like that.

When they loaded them out it was always at night, and we had to hand-catch them and put them in these small crates that they loaded on a semi-truck that was backed up in front of the barn. We would carry them all to that truck and this guy would take them and throw them in the crates. It probably took us three, four hours to get one floor loaded. It seemed like we started about three o'clock in the morning and worked until 7 or 8 a.m., and then we had to go to school so we couldn't even change clothes. But we weren't the only ones who smelled like chickens. Some smelled like cows. We all had our distinctive smells, I guess.

How the Tyler Street Farm was Purchased

The way Grandpa Martin originally bought the Tyler Street farm was quite a deal. Martin bought the farm from a guy named Maurice Luidens. That's who it was. He bought fifty-six acres from him. Martin thought that he bought the farm "as is," and that meant the silo was full when we bought it and he figured it should be full when he took it over. He come to take it over and the silo was empty.

Martin, he must have been a little short on patience, but he reneged on the deal. They both went to the same church and it was so bad that neither one of them would take communion, because you couldn't take communion if you had trouble with a brother in the church. This went on for a while and evidently they finally worked something out and then Grandpa bought the place. The title transfers that I saw indicate that Martin had bought it, then it went back to Maurice Luidens, and then it went back to Martin again. There was about a year in between there. That was quite an ordeal.

My son Brent has all those papers. I think this purchase went through in 1922, because 2022 is when Brent is going to go for a Centennial Farm plaque, that it's been in the family for 100 years.

The barn was built in 1897, but it is in a lot better shape today than it ever was when we had it, I think. I've done a lot of work there. I put in a whole section of second floor, I fixed that up. I put in a third floor in a section, and on that third floor I built a grain bin that they run feed into and gravity flows down to the cattle feeders on the first floor. I built all that stuff. I built all the gates in there. We poured a lot of cement in there too. Where the old cattle stanchions used to be for the milk parlor, I tore all that concrete out because it was so rough and we poured a whole new floor there.

Brent and I jacked up every beam, cut the bottom off, and poured cement pads under them because they were all settling so bad. Because they were just standing on those big field stones that they had underneath them. Huge, huge stones. We had one come up in the northwest corner of the barn, it started pushing up, so I dug it out with the tractor and it wouldn't fit in the bucket. Unbelievable. I don't know how those guys ever got those stones in that position. It's unbelievable how big they are. But the barn is in pretty good shape today.

The folks weren't very well-off when we were kids. I was born in 1947 and now I know they were struggling. But we didn't really realize that. We just figured that's the way it was. We knew quite a few families, especially in our church around South Olive, that were struggling. But there were some that were probably pretty well off, too. I'm sure there were.

When we were kids, the sleeping arrangements were tight. We had two bedrooms upstairs. The boys had the big bedroom, and Karen and Nancy had the little bedroom upstairs. We just didn't think nothing of it. Bob and I had a bed that we slept on, and there were springs sticking through the fabric in the middle. We always had to remember to stay on our side. If we rolled over we'd get stung by one of those springs sticking through the bed.

In the winter, we'd have snow drifts on the *inside* of the windows instead of the outside, because the windows were in such bad shape. But we just figured that was part of life, you know. We'd just heap on the blankets if we could.

In the winter, the folks had one of these old-fashioned LP gas furnaces in the floor. It was a big one, the register was maybe three feet long, maybe a little longer than that, by two or three feet wide. We'd get up in the morning and go downstairs, and all us kids would crowd onto that big register and we'd be pushing each other around because the one that was in the middle was the warmest. I'm sure the rest of the brothers and sisters would relate to that one.

We all started doing chores when we were five, six, seven years old probably. We had a corn crib and, on Saturdays in the winter, Dad would have us fill bags with corn. I recall that Nancy helped, all of us did. There were a lot of rats around. I remember Nance had an experience with rats. I don't remember exactly how it went, but I know she didn't fare very well with that deal.

Nancy replied: Ah yes! I remember it like it was yesterday. I was there along with Karen helping fill bags of corn. It was Karen! All of a sudden, mice were running all over and one ran right up Karen's pant leg! She was so little. She was crying not knowing what was happening. Can't remember exactly how, but Dad somehow managed to rid her of that mouse. Karen says she has no memory of this mouse incident. She doesn't even remember the corn crib next to the chicken house. Glad she doesn't remember, no mouse PTSD!

We filled the bags with corn so Dad could take them to the mill. Dad had to grind feed for the animals. I don't recall where he did that. I don't know if he did it the same day that we filled them, or if he did it during the week. He'd take it to the Harlem Mill, or to the Holland Mill, or one of them, and grind feed for the cows. We'd shovel it into bags and it was still on the cob. It didn't take long to fill ten bags, or fifteen, or whatever it was.

When Bob and I were in grade school, Dad went into the chicken business, raising caponettes. That was what they called this particular kind of chicken, it was bred for meat. It was our job to fill all the feeders and stuff like that every day. I can't remember how many of them there were, maybe two or three thousand of them. Somewhere around that number.

The idea with caponettes is they would get big real fast. They were pumping growth hormones into them at that time from Van Den Bosch Feeds. That's who Dad had a contract with to raise these chickens. They gave them all kinds of these growth hormones. I don't know what it was, but they'd grow real fast. I'm guessing three, four months maybe, and then they'd be ready for market. They were big chickens, not like Cornish hens or something, but bigger than that because they were raised for the meat, so they wanted them big.

As Dad mentioned, there were problems with the hormones so this enterprise didn't last long. I'm not really sure what kind of a hormone they were putting in there, but it was not the greatest.

Bob and I had to catch these chickens when they had to load them up. I think Nance and Marlan would help – I don't know if Marlan was around then too much at that time, but I know Nance helped. We always did it at night, in the dark, so you could just walk right up to them most of the time and catch them. A semi would come, and it was full of chicken crates. One guy would be on the semi, and you'd get maybe five to ten chickens in one hand and five in another hand and haul them to the front of the barn and hand them to the guy that was loading them. At our age, our hands would get so sore from hanging on to them things, and doing so many trips back and forth.

Dad had to try so many things to make money. They had dairy cows first, that's what I remember. And then he went into pigs, before the chickens. He had ducks, too, one time. I think he raised them for eggs. I faintly remember them. They were just on one side of the barn, the west side. Why there, I don't know. It didn't pan out real great. A lot of people don't like a duck egg. Maybe they hatched them and it was to grow more ducks, I don't know. I was pretty young then.

I want to say that we had the ducks when Uncle Roger was still living. I think a lot of things would be different today if Rog would have lived. I think Dad and him would have really gone places. Rog was the go-getter; he wanted to have the biggest farm around in this area. It was a real blow when he died.

Later in Dad's life, he got into pigs again. He and Bob started that whole thing. Boy, I couldn't tell you exactly when. After Bob was working with Dad for a couple of years, they were getting pretty big, and they asked if I wanted to get involved, so I did for a while. And then Brian was involved, too. We had quite an operation going there for a while.

Shoot, even Nancy's husband Tom got involved a little bit when Tom and Nance would come on weekends or whatever. Saturday was our day of cleaning all the pens out. Ol' Tom, he dug right in and helped. With his good clothes on.

I liked the farm work, I really did. Even though the work was hard. So often, we did things the hard way. Dad's land was so wet, always wet. And in the fall you had to get the corn off. Well, he didn't want to pay a neighbor guy with a big combine to come in and combine it. So we picked all the corn by hand. I mean, ten, twelve, fifteen acres. Dad worked nights, so he would go out there during the day and pick by hand. Bob and I would go out there whenever we weren't in school or doing something else, we'd go out there with that little Ford tractor and we had a little ramp on the back where we could put pickle crates, and we'd fill those pickle crates with ears of corn.

If you've ever picked corn by hand, you know how you crack the husk off the stalk. And if you do that continuously for hours and hours and hours, right between your thumb and your first finger, it gets so sore. It builds up some callouses. But we had fun. The reason why I always thought it was fun is how we got that tractor through the corn field: we'd get that thing loaded pretty full on the back, on that little ramp we called it, and the front wheels would come right off the ground, and you'd take off. You had to steer it with the brakes. You hit one brake or the other brake to keep the thing in line. Bob and I really enjoyed driving the tractor. You always wanted to drive because it was so much fun.

You look at that big field and you think, "Oh, my gosh. We'll never get it done." We'd just make a small dent every time we went out there. But we didn't regret doing the hard work. I mean, you'd be complaining a little bit, but hey, we just figured that's the way it was, so we had to accept that.

When we were really little, like four or five, in the fall Dad would shock corn, they'd stand shocks of corn out in the field. We'd ride behind the shocker; they'd have a tractor and then the shocker, and we'd hook onto a loop on the back end of the shocker. We had skids, or whatever we could find that would slide along behind it, and then we'd sit on those and ride. That was a blast. Making fun any way we could, just to keep our minds occupied.

And we did have fun. Dad didn't work all the time. Around the time when Marlan was about to graduate from high school, basketball was such a big deal in our area. It still is, but for us on Saturday, right after maybe noon or one o'clock, Dad would say, "We're not going to work anymore. We're going to go play basketball." We'd play basketball on that little barn floor in the front there by where the milk room used to be. We had a basketball net up there.

Dad always shot with both hands. Of course, Marlan, he'd use a one-handed jump shot. It would be Marlan against Dad and Bob and I, because we were just little yet. Marlan would win most of the time. But we enjoyed doing that. We looked forward to that. That wasn't every Saturday, but it was quite often in the winter. And Dad loved basketball. He and Mom always had their season tickets for Holland Christian High School games. They sat in the reserved seats up in the Civic Center, had their special spot.

Mom and Dad really enjoyed watching basketball and being at the games. None of us really played high school sports. We just didn't have time to do it. I guess we could have. Bob was in track. He ran for a few years. I wasn't in much of anything. I would play intramural sports during noon hour at high school. They had certain things going on just to keep the kids busy at noon hour. We used to play battle ball in the old gym: you had ten guys on one side, ten on the other, and you'd throw the ball as hard as you could and try to hit somebody. It was like a basketball, or a soccer ball, or something that size. Some kids, they didn't have very good arms, but some of us had a pretty good arm and that would smart if we got hit.

School was important, and Dad and Mom were strict about homework. But Dad pretty much knew, as we grew older, who was headed for higher education and who wasn't. Bob was about one of smartest, I think. That's my impression. He wanted Bob to go to college. He was headed that way, but he dropped out after the first year. I think that bothered Dad quite a bit. Nancy went through two years of junior college.

Marlan went to college after he was in the military. He went to some college in Lincoln, Nebraska, or somewhere out there. I'm not exactly sure. But when I was growing up, I think Dad knew I was not college material, which was okay with me. He didn't push it that much. I started working at Bil Mar turkey farms right out of high school. Actually, I started there before I was out of high school; I worked there part-time after school.

I was in the military for a couple of years during the Vietnam era. But I went to Germany, rather than Vietnam. The reason was that Marlan was in Vietnam at that time, and he wrote me a letter and said, "Hey, brothers don't have to be in a war zone at the same time." That's the whole story behind that movie, *Saving Private Ryan*. That's how I ended up in Germany.

Dad was always involved with the church. He was there all the time. He was Sunday School superintendent for, I'm guessing, ten to eleven years. He had it down pat, he did a pretty good job and I guess they wanted to keep him on. During Christmas time, we always did a Sunday School Christmas program and stuff like that. Certain classes had different things that they had to do, either sing, or read the Christmas story. But everybody got a bag of candy and an orange or an apple after the program. Back on the farm, us kids felt so lucky because we had to fill all those candy bags right at home, get them all ready for the Christmas program. We got our hands full of candy, and we kind of pocketed some of that stuff on our own without Mom or Dad seeing it. That was always a blast. We always looked forward to that. That candy was a big deal, oh man.

We had a lot of freedom. We could ride our bikes all over. I don't remember it too well, but Bob said that a couple times we rode our bikes all the way to Holland. And you try doing that now today, it's a pretty long way, and you've got bike paths and everything else, but we rode right down 120th and right into town.

We all had bikes. Marlan had a Schwinn. He always had the best bike. I don't know why that happened. It got down to Bob and I, we had those big, fat-wheeled bikes. I think they were from Huffy. Not those nice ten-speed bikes like Marlan had.

We had some pretty good equipment, like that blue Ford tractor he had. It was the English model, a little Ford Dexta. That was a nice tractor when we first got it. The main reason Dad got it, I think, was because he did custom baling in the summer when they had hay. He and Uncle Rog did that forever. They were doing that before I was even on the scene. They made money doing that all over the place. He had a nice New Holland baler that was pretty up-to-date.

He wasn't doing his novelty business anymore by the time I came along. In fact, all I remember of the Holland Ornamental and Novelty Company, or whatever the name was, is that one time he pointed out to me the building where the company used to be. It was right by where East Town Russ' is in Holland. The building is still there. It's on the other side of the road, a little farther out of town on Chicago Drive. There's a car dealership there now. That's where Marlan worked for years, but when it was a different dealership. I think it was Dad and Uncle Bill who had that novelty business.[116]

Editor's Note

During my sophomore year at Hope College, I spent the weeks of winter break 1983–4 on the farm with Grandpa and Grandma Nienhuis, helping Grandpa Bub make split-rail fencing from pine trees. We spent the days on his wooded property he called the ryeland, out near the corner of Tyler Street and U.S. 31. In the evenings, he would sit in his recliner in the living room, writing in a series of six-by-nine-inch writing tablets. When I asked what he was working on, he said he was writing down stories from his life. He had seen so much change, from plowing with horses to moon landings, which I had watched on TV in that same room with him. He asked me to read some of what he was writing.

The short passages that I read struck me as important. Grandpa Bub had lived his entire life on these two farms in Crisp – his farm with Grandma Dot on Tyler Street and his parents Martin's and Nellie's farm just a quarter-mile down the road – and here was an account of the history of this place and its people since the late-1800s. Reading this, I could feel how the struggle to work the land and build church-centered lives had not only shaped my own family, but also the larger society.

This is a Dutch story, an immigrant survival story, and a deeply American story. People get shot and talk to the dead, hearts are broken, the Great Depression brings suffering, yet faith and family – an enormous web of extended relations in Olive Township and beyond – are constantly bringing help and solace. In this environment of deep care, Bub writes with the conviction that things are always getting better. I love these stories. He said I might have to help him with this memoir one day, and I said I would.

Twenty years later, in January 2003, when Grandpa Bub was in a hospice facility, he handed over his notebooks to me and told me to "fix it up, make it sound good." Other uncles and aunts were there, and everyone sang. He was having trouble getting a good breath, but Grandpa put his head back and closed his eyes. He loved hearing that music.

I didn't touch these notebooks for years. Grandpa wrote exactly like he spoke, and when I read them, I heard the sound of his voice. They were a mess of stories put down as he remembered them and which he later recopied into a green Michigan State college notebook and tried to put in some kind of order, with dates and side-notes scribbled in the margins, but I didn't want to change a thing. I had always admired Grandpa Bub for his optimism and his faith and his belief in humanity. These stories had little to do with his own ego or his legacy; he simply trusted that this glimpse of history would interest other people. The church is a living history, with hundreds of years of the past actively impacting this current moment, and this family history he presented is the same: it is one story of how we arrived at right now. The way he told it was just fine with me.

Finally, after a lot of years, I acknowledged that he wanted me to use his edit notes to put it in some kind of order, so I did. I have kept his voice, his syntax, and his word choice as much as possible, because I love the sound of it. Occasionally I rewrote a sentence for clarity or to help a sequence make sense, and I some-times added dates in the text to help the reader know when things happened. Grandpa Bub's memory was remarkable, like Uncle Marlan's, too, but lots of things needed comment; I added end-notes with all kinds of dates and added information.

You will notice that these stories end when all the kids are married. Brian Nienhuis marries Marilyn Vork, and that's the last thing in the notebook, full stop. I think he meant to write more, but that's as far as he got. This history is pretty much strictly the farming and working lives of Bub and Dot and their children while they were all on the farm. So I kept the comments from the children of Bub and Dot to their farm days, too. It's a farm memoir.

Bub and Dot, however, have another history. They traveled all over the world. Bub notes in this book that their trip to Germany in 1970 to see Jack and Sue "got us started on our world trips."

I don't even know the full extent of their travels, but I know they went to India and to Egypt and to Machu Picchu in Peru. For farmers, they really got around. Bub talks a lot in this book about his cousin and best friend Chet Schemper, but does not mention that the Rev. Schemper later became Latin America Coordinator for the World Home Bible League (now The Bible League) and also oversaw Bible translations for Asia, Latin America and Africa. Chet said he traveled to fifty-nine countries to deliver Bibles in unusual translations, and occasionally Bub and Dot went along, where they were exposed to a mix of deluxe airline lounges and missionary work with very remote populations. None of these adventures are mentioned in his book. Maybe he was too busy living them.

I am grateful for the help of my mother, Nancy Wilson, for collecting photos, writing out her memories, verifying facts and finding sources, and sometimes reading Grandpa's challenging handwriting, and to my aunts and uncles, Marlan, Bob, Jack, Karen and Brian for similar contributions. Big thanks to cousin Marcia Lubbers for her excellent book about the Kooyers family, *Twisted Roads to the Past*; to the late Rev. Chet Schemper for his memoir, *Going Down Memory Lane*; and to Harold Vander Zwaag for his history of Olive Township, *Paging the Days of Olive*.

In 2000, Grandpa and Grandma came out to Southern California for the wedding of cousin Christopher Nienhuis and his bride, Kim. While they were in the area, we went to see the Rev. Robert Schuller's Sunday service at the Crystal Cathedral in Garden Grove. Schuller was a Hope graduate and a very well-known minister, and Bub and Dot watched his TV show, "Hour of Power." On the day we visited, Schuller invited to the pulpit a Muslim imam to discuss the shared texts and ideas of the Abrahamic religions. Grandpa thought this was great. "Isn't this wonderful?" he said as we filed out afterward. This kind of dialog was the way to understanding. That's the Bub I will always remember, open to new ideas, full of wonder.

– Dean Kuipers

163

Notes

All endnotes added by editor

1. Church services were conducted in Dutch in 1916, so Martin would most likely have read from either of two synod-approved Bibles in common use at that time: the Dutch *Statenvertaling* translation, or the English King James version. The Christian Reformed Church in North America approved the first new English translation, the American Standard Version, in 1926.

2. Marvin's wife, Dorothy, would rib him that he remembered things that happened before he was born.

3. Henry "Hank" and Antoinette "Nettie" (Kooyers) Hopp. Antoinette was Nellie's sister. They lived in Holland.

4. Pastor of South Olive CRC 1911–15.

5. Pastor of South Olive CRC 1916–1923.

6. Bub scribbled an illegible, six-word note in the margin here that seems to describe how the motor problems were addressed with a "gauge," but the rest can't be deciphered.

7. William Nienhuis, Martin's older brother.

8. Peter D. Van Vliet was pastor at South Olive CRC from 1923 to 1944.

9. Borculo CRC records say April 10, 1927.

10. Bub wrote a margin note indicating he thought it was 1929.

11. Bub wrote a margin note indicating he thought it was 1941. The fire was reported in *Holland Evening Sentinel*, March 18, 1941. The church was rebuilt and the dedication was set for Thanksgiving Day the same year, *Holland Evening Sentinel*, November 18, 1941. Hope College's Donald van Reken Local Newspaper Index (1872–1991).

12. Bub indicates in a margin note that it was 1946. Unconfirmed.

13. President Warren G. Harding died August 2, 1923. Bub was six at the time.

14. Bub's handwritten draft did not name him, but this older brother was Willard, known as "Bill."

15. Holland Christian High School was opened in 1922, according to *Holland City News*, August 18, 1921. A new Holland Christian high school building went into use in the fall of 1967, at its current location at 40th Street and Ottawa Ave; *Holland Evening Sentinel*, September 6, 1967. It was rebuilt in 1983 and updated since; *Holland Evening Sentinel*, August 24, 1983. Van Reken Index.

16. Muyskens coached Holland Christian to two state Class C championships, the last in 1934, then left in 1935 to coach for a decade at Calvin College.

17. Pantomime is a musical comedy stage production designed for family entertainment, in which the audience would join in singing songs or repeating call-and-response lines.

18. Meyer Music has been in business in Holland since 1872, but Bub is referring to a different building than the current building at 675 E. Lakewood Blvd.

19. Bub marked this passage as 1926 or 1927, so this could be one of several Mrs. Loomans. Clara and Harm Looman lived on the farm directly north of Martin Nienhuis, on the Northwest corner of 124th and Tyler. Clara was often at the Nienhuis homestead and Bub and Dot's kids remember walking over to visit her often, too. Harm's brother Gerrit Looman and his wife Diena (Stegeman) Looman lived just down Tyler at 112th, so it could also have been Diena, who died in 1928. Nellie (Kooyers) Nienhuis' sister, Johanna, who went by "Hannah," married Gerritt and Diena's son, Manley Looman, but they lived in Zeeland, so she wasn't really a neighbor. It could have been any one of them or even another who got a ride home, but it was probably Clara.

20. Bub calls it the "Patowonie area." Pottawattomie Park, Hofma Preserve and Hofma Park give access to the bayou today, but there could have been any number of places to stop in 1930.

21. Now M45 or Lake Michigan Drive.

22. Grand Rapids-based car company founded by Norman de Vaux, produced cars in 1931 and '32.

23. AAA insurance reported job and salary cuts in the early 1930s and lost 300,000 members, about a third of their enrollment, as the Depression began, but a declaration of bankruptcy could not be confirmed.

24. Eibeltje Workman

25. Eildert Nienhuis born December 12, 1849 in Eenrum, De Marne, Groningen, Netherlands.

26. Genealogical records indicate Martinus (often spelled Martynus) and Atje (often spelled Altje) had five children: three boys and two girls. Harmana, Eildert and Pieter were born in the Netherlands and emigrated. Abel and Martha were born in the U.S. Harmana died in the U.S. in 1860 at age 14.

27. There are discrepancies about the date of Martynus' death. *Genealogy of the Descendants of Eildert Markus Nienhuis*, which Bub owned and used as a reference, lists the date of death as 1890. Online genealogies such as Geni list the year of his death as 1896, which would have made him 76 or so. Listing managed by Jacob Berend Nienhuis, October 2, 2018; https://www.geni.com/people/Martinus-Nienhuis/6000000027257886090.

28. Here, Bub wrote the word "Reinders" in the margins. It may be a reference to Rick Reinders, a cousin his age he used to visit in Chicago and whom he mentions later in this text as being killed in World War II. Genealogy records indicate many relatives with the surname Reinders or Reenders woven into the Nienhuis past, and also into the Workman or Werkman families both in Groningen, Netherlands, and the Chicago area.

29. Eildert died March 23, 1921. His farm was a mile north of Martinus' farm and Brian and Marilyn Nienhuis live on acreage today that was part of Eildert and Emma's farm.

30. Online genealogical records list neither birth nor death dates for Eibeltje Workman (often spelled Werkman), which possibly reflects Bub's memory that she was an orphan.

31. Genealogical records list his name as Berend Willem Kooyers, but he was known as William or Will, and his birthdate is July 27, 1863. Gertie Meengs (also spelled Geertye and Gerritje) is listed as being born April 1, 1861, and the two of them were married August 14, 1883.

32. Bub lists this as 1890, but *Holland City News* notes this happened October 10, 1893. Nellie was nine in 1893. Marcia Lubbers, *Twisted Roads to the Past*, 93.

33. The first child of William and Gertie was still-born, but three others died in infancy. Lubbers, *Twisted Roads*, 27.

34. Date added for context. She died January 28, 1924 in Olive Township. "Gerritje Meengs died at her home in Crisp three weeks after breaking her hip in a fall. She was sixty-two years old. In 1921 she suffered from a stroke which left her unable to take care of herself. She relied on other family members to assist her in daily tasks." Lubbers, *Twisted Roads*, 26.

35. He would have been seven years old.

36. Bub did not name them, but it is common knowledge in the family that the aunt and uncle involved with spiritualists were Antoinette "Nettie" (Kooyers) Hopp, daughter of William and Gertie, and her husband Henry "Hank" William Hopp. This is confirmed in conversations with uncles and aunts who heard it directly from Bub, and through research by Marcia Lubbers and others. Hank and Nettie lived in Holland and one or both of them practiced as "divine healers." They later moved to Los Angeles, CA.

37. Bub added a margin note that this was 1926. Lubbers notes that it wasn't until 1928 that suspicion swirled that Gertie had been poisoned. Lubbers, *Twisted Roads*, 114.

38. It's unclear if they found anything in the feed. A jar of Paris green, an arsenic rodenticide and paint, was found buried in the yard by Ottawa County investigators. Lubbers, *Twisted Roads*, 114.

39. Hank and Nettie Hopp.

40. Lubbers' narrative helps clarify this story. Bill and Martha had moved back to the Kooyers farm to help take care of Gertie after her stroke in 1921. Bill and Martha had previously lived with Hank and Nettie Hopp in Holland. There was possibly bad blood between them, because Grandpa William, Hank and Nettie, and her sister Gezina ("Zena") accused Martha of the poisoning. Lubbers, *Twisted Roads*, 114.

41. Dutch translators say that "thick-neck people," translates here roughly as "arrogant" or "self-exalted." Basically, people who thought they had all the answers. Bub might be describing the spiritualists, or he might be describing Grandpa William as he behaved under their influence.

42. The reference to "Mrs. Kiekover" is most likely a simple error. After leaving the Kooyers farm, Aldert went to live with his sister Fannie, whose married name was Feenstra, at their home at 43 Taft Street, Zeeland. He died there in 1955. Fannie's oldest daughter was Anna Marie Feenstra, who married John Kiekover in 1920. It's certainly possible that Aldert lived with the Kiekovers some of the time, too, but most likely Bub is confusing Anna Marie with her mother Fannie. Lubbers, *Twisted Roads*, 25, 28.

43. Raymond worked at Limbert for quite a while. He and Eve Ellen married in 1943.

44. In fact, he lost the farm to foreclosure in 1927, according to newspaper accounts. The farm was owned by Albert Timmer of Zeeland and William lived there as a tenant. *Holland Evening Sentinel*, July 27, 1940.

45. According to the memoir of Rev. Chet Schemper, Grandpa William Kooyers never learned to drive. Rev. Chet Schemper, *Going Down Memory Lane*, 9.

46. Edema, or fluid buildup, due to congestive heart failure.

47. After moving from the Kooyers farm, Bill and Martha worked Martin Nienhuis' Tyler St. farm.

48. Bub does have an Uncle Harry Nienhuis, but this is probably Harry Schemper, who worked in town and drove to work with Bub's older brother Bill; it's later noted the Uncle Harry and Bill were also delivering the milk to the rusk factory for a while before Bub took over that job.

49. It has been reported as a ruptured appendix. Lubbers, *Twisted Roads*, 31.

50. Dr. Heyns' father, William, was a well-known professor at Calvin. Garrett Heyns' son, Dr. Roger Heyns, was later chancellor of the University of California, Berkeley.

51. Bub's hand-written notebooks included a copy of this poem that was apparently torn out of a Christian publication called *The Life Boat*, published by the Workingmen's Home and Life Boat Mission in Hinsdale, IL. Publication date unknown.

52. Dates that Bub had written in the margin added here for context.

53. Date added for context.

54. Wife of Harry Nienhuis, Martin's younger brother.

55. Baby Face Nelson added from news reports on WHTC radio and the *Holland Evening Sentinel*. He and accomplice Eddie Bentz reportedly got away with $70,000. https://whtc.com/2017/08/01/historic-downtown-holland-bank-to-reportedly-close/.

56. Date added for context.

57. "It was at the time the world's largest gray iron foundry, almost one mile from one end to the other. One day Henry Ford strolled through our department with company supervisors. We were laid off in 1938 because of an economic slump." Schemper, *Memory Lane*, 4.

58. Chet Schemper's tax return for 1937 shows income of $1509, most or all of which must have come from CWC. Badly needed money for those days. Schemper, *Memory Lane*, no page number.

59. The orchestra was called the Tulip City String Ensemble. From a newspaper report: "The Tulip City string ensemble of which Dean Mokma is director held a beach party at Buchanan Beach Wednesday evening. A wiener roast and hamburg fry was enjoyed. Those present were Mr. and Mrs. Dean Mokma, Mr. and Mrs. Howard Helder, Misses Margaret Stegink, Anna Bleeker, Grace Essenburg, Ida Belle Hieftje, Evelyn Steinfort, Jennie Ludema and Joe Ludema, Pete Ludema, Albert Kraker and Charles Kraker. Chet Schemper could not attend." "String Ensemble Has Party at Buchanan," *Holland City News*, July 13, 1939.

60. It was probably 1938 or '39, since he says earlier they went into business in 1938.

61. Family names added for context. Elizabeth spelled her nickname as Bette, but Bub and newspapers and others often misspelled it as Betty.

62. Bub's sentence was unclear, but either John Altena or Gabriel Kuite or both contacted them. John Altena was Dot's uncle, husband of Jenny Zuverink. Gabriel Kuite married Dot's sister Alice Van Langevelde.

63. Bub wrote "brother Clair," but the shortened version of the male Clarence would be "Clare."

64. Date added for context.

65. Details about Peter added, https://www.findagrave.com/memorial/49804463/peter-van_langevelde.

66. Added as an explainer because most people know her as "Hon."

67. The wedding date was announced at Dot's 18th birthday party, September 30, 1938, at the Martin Nienhuis home, as reported in an undated news piece about the celebration that looks like it came from *Holland City News* and was found in Bub's bible.

68. No confirmation of this name was found. From Bub's handwriting, it could be "Bermet" or "Bernet."

69. A newspaper account reports: "Miss Marion Mouw sang d'Hardelot's 'Because' before the ceremony. She was accompanied by Miss Faye Van Langevelde, who also played the bridal chorus from Lohengrin. Attendants were Miss Bette Marie Van Langevelde, sister of the bride, and Clifford Edwin." *Holland City News*, Dec 15, 1938. "Oh Promise Me" and "I Love You Truly" have been recorded together by many popular artists, most prominently Liberace.

70. Merrymakers who disrupt the wedding until the groom comes out to hush them with money or gifts.

71. Bub's penmanship is unclear here. He writes what looks like: "His supposedly know how didn't work," but the words "know how" are messy. Could be something describing a tool.

72. The Charles P. Limbert Furniture Co. was located in Holland. Bill's younger brother Ray Kooyers also worked there.

73. Local newspapers have many references to births at the Lampen Maternity Home. Van Reken Index.

74. Bub wrote what looks like "Damers," but Lester reappears further on in the narrative, and his family is confirmed here: https://ancestors.familysearch.org/en/MC86-FRY/lester-dams-1911-1986.

75. The nickname "Bud" could not be confirmed, but a John H. Van Til from Ottawa County was killed while fighting in the Pacific, listed November 28, 1942.

76. Date added for context.

77. Rev. Heyboer served at South Olive CRC from 1949 to 1958.

78. Dr. Minnema served at South Olive CRC from 1958 to 1962.

79. Bub and Chet Schemper returned to work at CWC, and Cliff and Roger soon worked there, too. "In the fall of 1942, I returned to Campbell, Wyant & Cannon Foundry Company, working on a high priority project for the U.S. Army and Navy.... I received automatic military deferments because of my work on the farm and also being involved in a high priority product at the factory where I worked." Schemper, *Memory Lane*, 4.

80. Bub added this date in the margin.

81. Rev. Henry A. Mouw served Sixth Reformed from 1949 to 1983.

82. Bub marked this as 1948–49.

83. The property he called the "ryeland" is at Tyler St. and 136th, near U.S. 31. The other property was nearby and, according to notes by Marlan, part of it may have been sold as a right-of-way for the expansion of U.S. 31 that began in 1950.

171

84. Here, Bub spelled the name Vandenburgh, but earlier wrote VandenBerg. Neither spelling could be confirmed, so VandenBerg was used for consistency.

85. Unable to confirm that cyanide was used as a hair-loss treatment, but perhaps he's referring to cyanamide. The popular hair-loss drug minoxidil, a vasodilator, is chemically derived from cyanamide, though I could find no evidence that cyanamide itself was used as such a treatment. Many drugs contain cyanide compounds, including some other vasodilators such as nitroprusside.

86. Date added for context; Marlan was in eighth grade in 1954–5.

87. A "capon" is a castrated rooster chicken. "Caponizing" roosters makes them grow especially heavy with meat and are considered more tasty. Much heavier than typical roasters, fryers or broilers, capons are sold around 8–10 lbs. and more. "Caponettes" refers to capons sterilized not with surgery but with estrogenic steroids (diethylstilbestrol) in injections or implants, which also made them grow heavy. The steroid practice was discontinued.

88. Bub spells it "Lescooly." Bub was also a devoted fan of TV exercise guru Jack LaLanne, and did a lot of LaLanne's workouts in the small basement on Tyler St.

89. Marlan graduated from high school in 1959.

90. Marlan was drafted in December 1963.

91. Name could not be confirmed.

92. Herman Van Langevelde died in 1960. https://www.findagrave.com/memorial/49804472/herman-van_langevelde.

93. Ruth Ann Schra Kuipers died in Holland Hospital May 16, 1964. She and Ron lived in Falls Church, VA, but she was the daughter of Mr. and Mrs. John Schra of Drenthe and had been visiting the family in Drenthe after the birth of her third child, Mitchell. https://www.findagrave.com/memorial/14668962/ruth-ann-kuipers.

94. New Year's Eve.

95. Bub wrote "eighty one," but according to Marcia Lubbers' book, Nellie Kooyers was born Jan 20, 1884 and died May 1, 1964, so she was 80. Bub's copy of *Genealogy of the Descendants of Eildert Markus Nienhuis* lists her death as April 28, 1964. Lubbers, *Twisted Roads*, 27.

96. Michelle Marie Nienhuis, born July 13, 1967.

97. Karen remembers that the tumor was described as being as big a football, so it must have been sixteen inches in circumference, or about five inches in diameter.

98. Date added for context.

99. Date added for context.

100. Sentence added for context. "Dorothy Nienhuis, 49, route 2, charged with negligent homicide in the death of Leonard Mastenbroek of Kalamazoo, who was fatally injured April 11 in a two-car crash at Beeline Rd. and U.S. 131, waived examination when arraigned in Holland District Court this morning and was bound over to Ottawa Circuit Court to appear May 11. Mastenbroek, 63, died two days later in Kalamazoo. He was a passenger in a car driven by Robert Ashbrook of Three Rivers. Ottawa sheriff's officers investigated." "Woman Bound Over In Negligence Case," *Holland Evening Sentinel*, April 20, 1970.

101. Bub's handwriting is unclear here, but it seems he meant William "Bill" Coupe. He was licensed as an attorney in 1966 and practiced in Holland and Saugatuck for over 40 years, finally as part of Coupe, Van Allsburg & Pater PC. He died in 2016.

102. Jack and Sue were married April 11, 1969.

103. Year added for context.

104. Bub may have been confused about seeing the "Gold Chamber." Berchtesgaden is the location of the Eagle's Nest, or Kehlsteinhaus, built by the Nazi party on a high mountain perch above town. Hitler rarely went there but it was massively built and was reached by a large, ornate elevator of brass and Venetian mirrors, which can still be seen. Berchtesgaden was also the location of Hitler's summer home, Berghof, which he remodeled himself with money from the sale of *Mein Kampf*, and this is where he spent a great deal of time with his longtime girlfriend and eventual wife, Eva Braun. According to a 1938 story in the UK *Homes & Gardens*, it was not ornately decorated but had a light and airy feel, though the great hall did have a large red marble fireplace mantel. The Gold Chamber is probably another term for the fabled Amber Room, which, according to *Smithsonian*, was an extraordinary room with walls of amber backed by gold, gifted to Peter the Great in 1716 and looted from Russia by the Nazis in 1941. It was shipped to Königsburg (now Kaliningrad), but it was not a hangout for Hitler. The boxed wall panels disappeared from Kaliningrad in 1943 and have never been found.

105. Possibly the Texas Ranger Hall of Fame and Museum in Waco, TX, with its firearms collection.

106. John W. Maas was pastor at South Olive CRC 1972–1983.

107. Roger G. Timmerman was pastor at Middleville CRC 1973–2001.

108. Married June 8, 1974.

109. Marlan ran logistical operations for the region from a repurposed missile base near Coraopolis, and was an advisor to National Guard units in PA and WV.

110. Married Oct 22, 1976.

111. William Nienhuis, born Aug 12, 1876.

112. Arthur Nienhuis, MD, went on to work at the National Institutes of Health and become the fourth director and CEO of St. Jude Children's Research Hospital in Memphis. A noted hematologist and gene therapy pioneer, he died February 3, 2021. A very fine tribute was posted on the St. Jude website: https://blogs.stjude.org/progress/gene-therapy-pioneer-led-st-jude-through-unprecedented-growth/

113. The name "Cannoni & Sons" could not be confirmed, but Marlan has an exceptional memory, so perhaps they were subcontractors. According to Michigan State Highway Dept. maps, in 1950 the route of U.S. 31 between Holland and West Olive was rebuilt and changed to more northwesterly route. *Michigan Official Highway Map* (Map), [c. 1:918,720], (April 15, 1950 version and July 1, 1951 version). Lansing: Michigan State Highway Department. § L8. OCLC 12701120.

A 1954 newspaper story details work on the stretch of U.S. 31 from Muskegon to Holland; a section "near West Olive" was graded by John and Paul Gillisee of Grand Rapids, and finished in June 1953. "In October, 1953, the final paving contract was awarded to Carl Goodwin and Sons of Allegan for $378,467.39. This included a 22-foot strip concrete road 6.2 miles long. The single strip road will link up with other sections completed in recent years." "Highway Construction Marks Peak For Holland Area During Past Year," *Holland Evening Sentinel*, Jan 4, 1954.

114. In the landmark 1962 case, *Engel v. Vitale*, the U.S. Supreme Court decided six to one that school-sponsored prayer in a public school was unconstitutional. Similar cases quickly followed, determining that school-sponsored Bible readings were also unconstitutional.

115. Clara Raak Looman was born in 1866, so Nancy would have known her in her 80s and 90s. https://www.findagrave.com/memorial/113961317/clara-looman.

116. The Holland Ornamental and Novelty Works was run by Bub and cousin Chet Schemper.

www.ingramcontent.com/pod-product-compliance
Lightning Source LLC
Chambersburg PA
CBHW070205060426
42445CB00033B/1548